Ready to Answer

Ready to Answer

Why "Homophobic Church" is an Oxymoron

Rev. Marilyn Bowens

AuthorHouse™
1663 Liberty Drive
Bloomington, IN 47403
www.authorhouse.com
Phone: 1-800-839-8640

First published by AuthorHouse 08/05/2011

ISBN: 978-1-4634-4811-0 (sc)
ISBN: 978-1-4634-4810-3 (hc)
ISBN: 978-1-4634-4809-7 (ebk)

Library of Congress Control Number: 2011914001

Printed in the United States of America

This book is printed on acid-free paper.

Contents

Essays

Selected Sermons

ACKNOWLEDGEMENTS AND DEDICATION

Many people in my life have contributed, in some way, to the inspiration, insights, and experiences that led to my writing this book. I could never name them all. I hope that those who are not named will understand that, and know how much I appreciate you all. There are some, however, that I must acknowledge by name.

I am grateful for the spiritual foundation that I received as I was raised in the United Holy Church of America, Inc.; and particularly, Faith Tabernacle U.H.C.A. in Washington, DC. It was there that I came to know God as One with whom I could have a personal relationship. I had many examples of what it means to put God first in one's life; to make doing God's will one's highest priority. Though some of you, no doubt, think that I have made a drastic departure from the values instilled in me there, I hold fast to that which you gave me which is most important. I thank you for it; and I pray to see the day when we all can agree that the things that we still have in common vastly outweigh our differences.

To the Metropolitan Community Church; and particularly, St. John's MCC in Raleigh, NC, and MCC-New Haven: St. John's, thank you for being my church home. Thank you for being a place of healing and restoration for me. Thank you for embracing me—all of me—without requiring me to hide or deny any part of who I am in order to be welcomed at Christ's table among you. Thank you for participating in the discernment of my call to ministry; and for your support, on which I know I can rely to this day. Thank you,

MCC-New Haven, for your willingness to take a chance on a brand new pastor, before the ink was dry on my license! The opportunity that you gave me has resulted in so much growth; so much learning that comes only through experience. Your place in my life story, and my heart, is sealed forever.

To The Fellowship of Affirming Ministries: Thank you for paving the path that has led me back to my Pentecostal roots! I know that God led me to you; and I am excited to see how my journey with you will unfold!

To Rev. Elder Troy Perry, Rev. Dr. Nancy Wilson, Bishop Yvette Flunder, Mother Shirley Miller, Rev. Wanda Floyd, and Rev. Brenden Boone: You are my heroes and "she-roes"! Each of you, in the course of your ministries, have inspired me, taught and mentored me, and enabled and empowered me to see possibilities that I did not know existed. You each, in your own way, changed my life; and brought me one step closer to the fulfillment of God's purpose for my life. Thank you!

To my sister, Jo: There are no words. Really. I just wouldn't know where to begin. I have to trust that you know.

To my sisters, Sheila and Carla: Thank you for the knowledge I have always had that, when all is said and done, you will be there and you will have my back!

To my sons, J.T. and Trey: I have always called you "the eternal loves of my life." You always will be.

To BJ: We saved the best for last, didn't we? Thank you for your love, your companionship, your encouragement, and your support. I am blessed to have you as my partner.

I dedicate this book to the memory of my parents—Bishop Joseph Thomas Bowens and Mother Clara Washington Bowens—with all of the love my heart can hold. I minister to many people who lose everything, including the love of their parents, when they come out as lesbian, gay, bi-sexual, or transgender. Both of my parents knew exactly who I am long before they died. And both of them made sure that I *know* that they loved me no less. For this, and for everything I received from them that I cannot adequately articulate, I am deeply and eternally grateful.

Love to you all —
Marilyn

INTRODUCTION

1 Peter 3:14-16 (KJV):

[14]But and if ye suffer for righteousness' sake, happy are ye: and be not afraid of their terror, neither be troubled; [15]But sanctify the Lord God in your hearts: and be ready always to give an answer to every man that asketh you a reason of the hope that is in you with meekness and fear: [16]Having a good conscience; that, whereas they speak evil of you, as of evildoers, they may be ashamed that falsely accuse your good conversation in Christ.

There is a principle that I live by that I call "redeeming the pain." That is my way of expressing my belief that something good can come out of any pain we experience. The basis for that belief is Romans 8:28—"We know that all things work together for good for those who love God, who are called according to his purpose." Looking for ways to bring good out of my pain is what I call "redeeming the pain." To the extent that I can do that, I am relieved of the feeling that I went through whatever I went through for nothing.

I find that sharing our stories is often a way to redeem our pain. Those experiences that sear our souls, the ways that we find of getting through them, and the insights that we gain in the process, are often exactly what another person needs; sometimes what another person is desperate for, to get through their own experience of similar pain.

I feel inspired to write this collection of essays and musings with a few hopes and prayers in mind. First, my prayer is that Christians of minority sexual orientation and/or gender identification and expression will find hope, comfort, peace, and freedom from the torment of "the Accusers." "The Accusers" is my label for those in Christian churches who persist in refusal to affirm and embrace us as the full-fledged, equally beloved children of God and members of the Body of Christ that we are. I know that pain. I am on a journey that has taken me through fear of loss of my soul, because of one aspect of who I am that I did not choose and cannot change, to the blessed assurance of God's unconditional and eternal love for me. It took a while to get through the torturous part of the journey. But I did, with the help and by the grace of God. I want others on that path to know that the same help and grace are available to them. It would redeem my pain if this book conveys that to one person.

I also pray that this work will find its way into the hands of our Christian allies and those of "straight" Christians who are asking the hard questions and engaging in the difficult conversation about whether faithfulness to Christian faith allows for the full inclusion of people who are lesbian, gay, bi-sexual or transgendered in their churches. It does; in fact, it requires it. I am grateful for all who have engaged in that conversation without investment in protecting the status quo in most churches, but with sincere desire to discern and do God's will. It will redeem my pain if this book assists even one of you in embracing and helping others to embrace an understanding of God's love as radically inclusive of all of humanity.

Finally, I pray that some Accusers will, somehow, be led or persuaded to read this book. Even if their original intent is to chew it up and spit it out; to play "scripture war games," pitting each reference to scripture that I make against one that they choose to "prove" me wrong, I hope some will read this. Why? Because I trust the Holy Spirit to bear witness to truth. And I trust that, even if they start reading this with the intent of refuting it and discrediting me, God is able to change their hearts, minds, and intentions by the time they reach the end of it. I have no illusions—that will not be the case for all of them; probably not even most. But it would redeem the pain I have borne if this book plays any part in there being even one less Accuser in this world inflicting that same pain on other LGBT Christians.

My intent is to speak in my own voice, from my own experience, in a way that will be accessible to many people. There is a lot of readily available published material in which gifted Bible scholars—LGBT and straight—exegete scripture, do word studies, mine and compile historical information and present eloquent arguments for the full inclusion of LGBT's in the life of the church. I am grateful for their work. It is not my intent to write a weak imitation of that kind of scholarship. What I hope for is to engage whoever will read this in holy conversation about the topics herein; sharing my thoughts and stimulating thought in them.

I am who I am. God created who I am. I am standing fast in the liberty wherein Christ has made me free. No more apologizing; no more arguing; no need to defend. But if anybody asks me, sincerely wanting information about the basis of my hope in Christ, I am finally ready to answer. The rest, I leave in God's most capable hands.

Rev. Marilyn Olivia Bowens

ESSAYS

RELIGION OR RELATIONSHIP?

Spoon-feeding is for babies, not maturing Christians. The problem I have with religion, as practiced in many churches, is that there seems to be an expectation (at best) or a requirement (at worst) that fully-grown adults allow ourselves to be spoon-fed the church's religion of choice. They say, "Know God for yourself." But it seems that they really mean, "Know *what we tell you* about God for yourself." That placed me squarely between the proverbial rock and hard place. Doing what they expected me to do was precisely what made it impossible for me to do what they told me to do.

I grew up in a religious system that did not encourage independent thinking on theological matters. My sense is that many churches operate the same way. They are "right." They know and teach "the truth." If you have a *permissible* question, they have *the* answer. If they don't have an answer, that's only because the question was not permissible in the first place. Some things are simply not to be questioned. Some people are simply not to be questioned.

What a dilemma for anyone who loves the Lord with all of his or her heart, and after (or while) growing up in a church that embraces Accuser-theology, comes to understand that s/he is LGBT! If you continue to allow yourself to be spoon-fed their "religion," you must accept that you must change something about yourself that you cannot change or go to Hell. The only other slightly more humane choice some Accuser-churches offer is to renounce homosexuality and refrain from "practicing." You have a shot at getting to Heaven, and having a marginal place in the life of the church until then, if you accept being sentenced to a life of involuntary celibacy. You must deny yourself satisfaction of all of those quintessentially human social, emotional, and sexual longings that are fulfilled in loving intimate partnerships and marriages. For most people, this is not really a humane option at all; just the lesser of the evils, given the choices.

When I preach, I often explicitly point out the "take-away thought" of the sermon. This is the main thing that I understand to be the message to be conveyed; the thing that I want to be sure that everyone hears. The take-away thought of this essay is: *Authentic faith and personal relationship with God absolutely require giving yourself permission to ask your questions.* Many Accuser-dominated religious systems won't give us that permission. And there are reasons for that. But we have the power to give it to ourselves; and the right to ask the questions.

I'll share some thoughts about why Accuser-churches don't like questions, and then some thoughts about why LGBT Christians must ask them. I do not suggest that all of these reasons apply to all Accuser-churches. These are observations and musings from a number of different places I have been.

Let's get the more cynical (but, in some cases, real) reasons out of the way first. In the kind of churches I'm talking about now—churches with rigid theology and requirements of strict conformity in thinking—there is a power structure that depends on keeping everyone on the same page. In some churches, most (if not all) of the power is vested in the pastor; who is perceived as having a "hot line" to the Lord, vastly superior to anyone else's connection to God. What the pastor says goes, because the pastor is "God's mouthpiece" reporting, verbatim, what God has told him or her. So to question the pastor is tantamount to questioning God. Disagreeing with the pastor is out of the question. Some of these pastors, and the people who follow them, are good and sincere people, "doing church" in the only way they know; the way that they fervently believe is how it should be done. I am not judging their intentions. I am describing the system that they perpetuate. That system requires passive acceptance of what they say about God, about what God does and does not like, about what it means to "live right."

The leaders of these religious systems do not have the luxury of being wrong; certainly not very often and not about anything really important. If you have ever been a part of one of these systems, think about it—How often do you hear these pastors say, "I was wrong;" or "I made a mistake;" or "I'm sorry" in reference to a theological stance? After they have spent years declaring, for example, that homosexuality is an "abomination," *in many cases without even knowing exactly what that word means*, and claiming that they got that directly from the Lord, how easy would it be for them to reverse themselves? They can hardly even afford to question their own understandings; to be open to new information and different insights; at least, none that are inconsistent with what they have been preaching for years. What would that do their credibility with their congregations? How quickly would their power go flying out of their stained-glass or store-front windows? Theological and policy reversals have huge potential to split a church. Pastors in these church systems cannot tolerate questions with the potential to lead to that result. So they do not. Since, typically, they are very charismatic leaders; they are surrounded by devoted followers who are just as invested in keeping them on their pedestals as they are in staying there; most often, because each and every one of them completely believes that, by perpetuating the status quo, they are doing the will of God.

Then, for some, there are issues of pride and privilege—the desire to hold onto heterosexual privilege magnified exponentially by an unfortunate tendency toward pride in their own "righteousness." Quiet as it is kept, there are, among Christians, some folks who simply enjoy feeling that they are "better" than others. For as long as they believe that they are living right and we are not, they are better than we are in their own eyes, and in the eyes of God. After all, right is always better than wrong. Most Accusers that I know maintain a deliberate distance from "the world," meaning things, people, and concerns that they deem to be "worldly." In some cases, that means pretty much anything that does not typically happen in church. So most of the ones I have known are not rich, not powerful, not stand-outs in society. Feeling spiritually superior probably means a lot more to them than even they realize.

Nonetheless, if I assume (which I choose to do) that most of these Accuser pastors and congregations are sincere in their efforts to please God, wouldn't that outweigh any concerns about admitting that they have been mistaken about us? Wouldn't at least some of them be compelled to consider the possibility; and to engage, however skeptically at first, in the conversation going on in many churches as they re-examine this issue? My sense is that there must be other reasons—even more compelling reasons—for their refusal to entertain the thought that the phrase, "LGBT Christian" is not an oxymoron.

I think I've seen, at least, two other reasons in my journey. The Accusers are extremely invested in being "right." Not just right about this issue; right with God. I want to be right with God, too. The difference is that the Accusers live in a two-toned theological environment. There is only black and white; right and wrong. There are no grays; and gray is the "color" of uncertainty. There is no room for uncertainty around things that matter; the things that they believe can cost you your soul. You're right or you're wrong, and since being wrong seals the fate of your eternal soul, you have to know that you are right. Doubt and uncertainty are enemies of the soul; as much a threat as being wrong. So Accusers have to *know* what they know; and we have to know what they know in order for us to be right.

The other thing that may explain the Accusers' tenacity in keeping their minds closed is closely related. Remaining faithful to the religious teachings that they have spoon-fed you insulates you from the dangers and pitfalls of thinking for yourself and trusting your own experience. A favorite proverb of some Accusers appears, in almost identical form, both at Proverbs 14:12 and 16:25. I present it as written in the King James Version of the Bible, because that is how I have heard it quoted most often: "There is a way that seemeth right unto a man, but the end thereof are the ways of death." Translated into Accuser-speak: "There is no quicker or surer way to lose your soul than to question what we have taught you and think theologically for yourself."

So, to be fair, it is not all about power, pride, and privilege for all of them. For some, it is also about deep and profound fear—the fear of being wrong; the fear of being "in error;" the fear that making a mistake, by thinking for themselves, could get them sent straight to Hell.

I have compassion toward people whose understanding of God strikes that kind of fear in their hearts, because I used to be one of them. The Bible presents God in a lot of ways, in various passages, and some of them are pretty scary. Those are not the images of God that dominate my understanding of God; based on my experience of God. "God is love" (1 John 4:8b) is the best description of God as I know God.

I believe that any good thing that I can do, God can do better. I have two sons who are the eternal loves of my life. I love my sons in a way that would never allow me to treat them the way that some Accusers believe God to be capable of treating God's children. I trust the saving work of God, manifested in the life, death, and resurrection of Jesus. I trust my faith in Him, and my acceptance of Him as my personal Savior, to make it safe for me to risk error by settling for nothing less than a personal and authentic relationship with God. I remember a sermon I heard someone preach during which he or she said something like, "When God looks at us, God looks through the lens of the saving work of Jesus and does not see our sins, shortcomings, and failures. God only sees our faith in God's Son." I do not believe that my sexual orientation is a sin, a shortcoming or a failure. But IF, for the sake of argument, I am in error about that, I know that God knows it is just that—error; not willful disregard of God's will for my life. I have prayed too hard, cried too much, studied too diligently, and begged too desperately for God to correct and change me, if I am wrong, to be able to believe that God would refuse to do that and then send me to Hell for being in error. I could say I believe that, because the Accusers say I should. But, in my heart of hearts, the simple truth is I do not. It does not ring true for me, because I am a better parent than that. And anything I can do, God can do better. So there would be no value in pretending that I believe that; because God, who knows my heart, would know that I would be lying.

When we are ready to choose relationship with God over passive acceptance of every aspect of the religion that we have been spoon-fed, it is best to start by telling God whatever is true. Relationships built on lies generally do not fare well. And what could be more futile than lying to God? If you have doubts about what you have been taught, you have them; and God knows that you do. If you have questions that you "know better" than to ask the folks around you, the questions are still there even if you do not ask them; and God knows that they are. If there is something about you that renders you organically incapable of being "right," as your spoon-fed religion defines "right," when you profess and pretend to be "right" by that standard, God knows that you are lying. "God is spirit, and those who worship [God] must worship in spirit and truth." (John 4:24) When you are ready to seek authentic faith and personal relationship with God, start by telling God the truth. And proceed to ask your questions. Read. Study. Seek out points of view other than those you have been hearing all of your life. Do not be afraid to question the Accusers' beliefs. Do not be afraid to question God.

I owe an eternal debt of gratitude to David, the psalmist. I love him. David left us a stellar example of a human being in real, authentic relationship with God. David told God the truth. He told God how he felt, what he loved, what he hated, what he wanted. When he was happy, he wrote psalms of praise; and when he was angry at God (yes, angry at God), he ranted and railed and threw tantrums. And David questioned God over and over again. God didn't smite him with a bolt of lightning for any of it.

I relate to God in much the same way. I tell God the truth. I approach God from wherever I am, in a given moment; just as I am. For me, that is the definition of real, personal relationship. And the faith that is evolving from that relationship is *authentic*. It is not spoon-fed religion. It is not passive acceptance and rote repetition of things I have been taught. It is me relating to God, and God engaging me and relating right back in ways I never would have imagined possible when I was trying to live by the religious "script" of others. I have been amazed to discover that the quickest way for me to get over being angry at God is to tell God that I am angry and throw my little tantrums. When I go the denial route, and walk around seething with unexpressed anger, disappointment, fear, or frustration, those emotions operate like a clog in a drain. It gets difficult to feel God, to hear God, to even want to talk to God. But when I learned to allow myself to relate to God, in an honest and real way, it turned out that no good tantrum goes unanswered. Not with lightning or in any other punitive way; in ways for which I am deeply and humbly grateful. I have reached the point where I think of these venting sessions as going to God for an attitude adjustment; because that has consistently been the result. Just like what we see in most of David's psalms. Even when they start with ranting and railing, they end with re-affirmations of faith and praise. It is the experience of that kind of relationship with God that has transformed my life and made my faith *my* faith.

With more clarity than ever before, I see what I have intuitively sensed for a while now—that for me, as a Christian, my gayness is a gift. Without it, I might never have questioned the exclusionary dogma, tradition, and practices perpetuated in the name of Christianity in the distorted forms to which most of us are exposed today.

Being part of the "insiders" in the church lulls people into a conviction of their own righteousness. Their conformity (real or feigned) with whatever their church says a Christian ought to be affords them the privilege of being comfortable oppressors of those who do not conform. For them, the system ain't broke; so they can live their whole lives in peaceful denial that anything about it needs fixing. It is because of my gayness that I do not have that luxury. Without my gayness forcing me to question and to seek; forcing my heart and mind to be open to new understandings, I might very well be one of those Christians passively accepting and adhering to hand-me-down religion, rather than being in active, authentic, challenging, dynamic, torturous, sublime, life-sustaining and soul-saving relationship with God.

When, as a child, I was taught that God loves me, I accepted that as true. My acceptance was based on trust and confidence in those who taught me that; not faith in God. How do I know? Because when I came out as a lesbian, and knew that nothing could entice some of those same people to bear witness to God's love for me anymore, I was no longer sure of it myself. Today, *no one* can shake my assurance of God's unconditional and eternal love for me; because it is not based on spoon-fed religion. It is based on my experience of real and personal relationship with God. It just does not get any better than that.

NEITHER "LIFESTYLE" NOR CHOICE

The importance and impact of the choice of words used to describe us cannot be underestimated. Words carry and convey much more than their literal meanings. There are often implicit connotations attached which, when spoken and internalized, can have effects of which we aren't consciously aware. That is the basis for my objection to referring to homosexuality as a "lifestyle."

First of all, it is not accurate. A "lifestyle" can be chosen or acquired or lost or relinquished. Being rich and famous is a lifestyle. Being a vegetarian is a lifestyle. Communal living is a lifestyle. Monogamy, polyamory, and promiscuity are all lifestyles practiced among heterosexuals and LGBT's alike. Homosexuality is not a lifestyle. It is a sexual orientation; an immutable characteristic. One is homosexual or not. It is not a choice.

I do not think it is accidental that many Accusers love to refer to "the homosexual lifestyle." And it saddens me to hear many LGBTs refer to our so-called "lifestyle." That word implies choice; or at least, a characteristic that we could (or God would) change if we were willing.

I never made a choice to be a same-gender-loving woman. I know a lot of LGBTs; have talked to and counseled too many to count. And I have never met one who said he or she chose his or her sexual orientation or gender identity. I think it is significant that I am immersed in a church setting to which most people come from other church settings. There could hardly be a more deeply ingrained aversion to being LGBT than the indoctrination that most of us received during our formative years. In other words, we would be among the very last people on Earth to choose to be anything other than heterosexual. We did not choose to be LGBT. I cannot count the stories I have heard of people's efforts to change their sexual orientation from gay to straight—everything from counseling to begging God to change them; from marrying and trying to "fake it 'til they make it" to attempted suicide; thinking it better to feel nothing than to feel their attraction to people of the same gender.

The thing that I find interesting is that the Accusers insist that homosexuality is a choice, even though they did not choose to be straight. Whether they admit it or not, they understand the power of their own sex drives. They know what it is to, literally, be *driven*, at some point, to seek satisfaction of their own needs for intimacy for which they have longings too intense to ignore. They didn't choose to have those longings and they didn't choose the objects of their attractions. The males among them did not choose, when their adolescent hormones were running amok, to have those involuntary erections that mortified them and turned them into contortionists in their efforts to hide them. Those, male and female, who struggled to repress all sexual feelings, in the name of holiness, did not choose to have the dreams through which their "nature" found some form of nocturnal expression despite their best efforts. And some of the Accusers know, all too well, that they did not choose their own attractions to people of the same gender that they would rather die than acknowledge.

Most people have probably experienced being attracted to someone to whom they would rather not be attracted. Most have probably also experienced not being attracted to someone who cared for them and whose feelings they wished they could return, but the "spark" or "chemistry" just was not there. If Accusers would give it just a little unbiased, honest thought, they would realize that sexual attraction *just is*, for all of us. It is not something we choose. Behaviors, for the most part, can be chosen and controlled. Feelings—not so much. And, "practicing" or not, it is the state of being attracted to the same gender, or to both, for sexual intimacy and/or romantic connection that manifests one's homosexual or bi-sexual orientation. We can choose to be sexually active or not. We do not—whether gay or straight—choose the gender(s) to which we are naturally attracted.

I admit to having made some choices about my sex life. I could have chosen to sentence myself to a life without romantic companionship and sexual intimacy. I chose not to do that. Or I could have chosen to be a perpetual liar; pretending to be straight while having secret liaisons with like-minded women. I chose not to do that either. I chose, instead, to face what is real and true about me and natural to me. I chose to ask God, rather than people, whether God loves me as I am. And once I knew that God's answer to that is "Yes, absolutely," I chose to embrace myself, and a life of integrity blessed with the gifts of loving companionship and sexual intimacy.

I chose to stop attending and supporting any church that has not demonstrated the humility to entertain the thought that *they* might be the ones "in error" on this subject; and that continues to wound and alienate God's LGBT children by denying our status as part of the Body of Christ. I chose to stop punishing myself for being myself by allowing them to use the Bible to abuse me.

I chose, in short, to worship God in spirit *and in truth.*

WHAT IS AN "ABOMINATION," ANYWAY?

The Accusers love to tell us, "The *Bible* says, 'It's an *abomination*!'" Most of them seem to believe that the word "abomination" is synonymous with "sin." It isn't. The Hebrew word translated as "abomination" is "*toevah*." It was always understood to be a relative term that meant that a particular act or practice was against the norms or acceptable conduct of a given society or group. It does not mean "sin" in the absolute sense of a transgression in the eyes of God.

The way that the word "*toevah*" is used in the Bible clearly supports this understanding of its meaning. It is used in the Old Testament over 100 times; only twice with reference to same-gender sexual conduct. Both of those instances appear in the law codes in Leviticus—a special group of laws given to the Israelites for the specific purpose of distinguishing them from their idol-worshipping and pagan neighbors. Any meaningful study of those laws reveals the high number and wide variety of things that are called an abomination *for Israel, in that day and time.*

Eating shellfish and wearing fabrics composed of more than one material are just two examples of abominations, according to those laws, that modern-day Accusers acknowledge to be obsolete and/or intended specifically for ancient Israel. Their acknowledgement that some of those laws do not apply to us today should, at least, give rise to some doubt about whether the one that they isolate and use against us is still applicable. What perplexes me is why they are so unwilling to give us the benefit of that doubt.

The understanding of *toevah* as a relative term is further supported by several of the verses in which the word appears. The

Bible speaks of certain things as an abomination to the Israelites, but not the Egyptians; others as an abomination to the Egyptians, but not the Israelites. It speaks of abominations "to the righteous," "to the wicked," and "to fools." Several of the abominations are stated to be "abominations to the Lord," as opposed to a given society. Notably, the two in Leviticus, so often misused against LGBT's, are not.

The implications of understanding abomination as a relative term are huge. What is an abomination to some is not to others. What a group of people deems to be an abomination at one point in time may not be deemed an abomination at another point in time by that same group. And at least some of what the Bible says God called an abomination, in those laws given specifically to Israel as a young nation, is properly understood, by Christians and Jews today, not to be abominations for us. Even the Accusers can't argue with that; given that they partake in or practice many of those abominations today without a pang of guilt.

While preparing for a Bible and Homosexuality class at my church, I looked up "abomination" on dictionary.com, just out of curiosity. In the definition there, this example is given: "Spitting in public is an abomination." I have never heard an Accuser suggest that anyone is going to Hell for that. This example illustrates that an abomination is whatever a given group or society says it is, at any given time or place, based on their understanding (or lack thereof) of the activity. It does not mean the same thing as "sin."

There was a time when it made some sense for the Accusers to see homosexuality as an abomination. In addition to their literal, out-of-context interpretations of a handful of scriptures, they had the medical establishment and the law of the land on their side. But in light of the state of knowledge about homosexuality, today—knowledge that gave rise to the medical establishment's renunciation of its original stance on the subject and is fueling the inevitable nation-wide change in the law, as well as the ongoing conversation in every major religious group in this country—it makes no sense at all for the church, of all institutions, to still be holding out. No more sense than it would make for them to condemn people to Hell for eating shrimp or wearing polyester.

ADAM AND EVE AND STEVE

It may look, for a minute, like my mind has wandered off the subject. Bear with me. There is a point, and we will be there shortly.

Before entering vocational ministry, I was an Assistant Professor of Law at my alma mater, North Carolina Central University School of Law in Durham, NC. My area of specialty was Constitutional Law. Each year, I taught my classes the landmark Supreme Court case, *Loving v. Virginia*. It is the case where the U.S. Supreme Court declared a state law that prohibited interracial marriage to be in violation of the U.S. Constitution; thereby prohibiting all states from enforcing similar laws. The Court reversed the decision of a lower court that had upheld the discriminatory law. The lower court's opinion contained the following explanation of the judge's reasoning:

> *Almighty God created the races white, black, yellow, Malay and red, and he placed them on separate continents. And but for the interference with his arrangement there would be no cause for such marriages. The fact that he separated the races shows that he did not intend for the races to mix.*

After reading the above excerpt to my classes, I would pose the following question:

> How is it that God Almighty, the Creator of the universe, who could fashion human bodies out of dust and breathe life into what was lifeless; who by speaking the word

> caused the waters to part and form oceans, thereby exposing the dry land that became the continents; God who, according to this judge, created the black people in Africa, and the white people in Europe, and the yellow people in Asia, and the red people in North America; God who sees all things and knows all things past, present and future—how is it that this same God did not take into account that someday somebody would invent . . . *the boat*?!

"The fact that [God] separated the races shows that [God] did not intend for the races to mix." That is an example of deductive reasoning; tragically faulty deductive reasoning. Today, most people find this to be a ridiculous statement. It is the underlying thought process to which I wish to call attention.

This judge looked at one single scriptural fact; one act of God as presented in the Bible, and took the flying leap from that point to a conclusion that purports to state God's intention for all people, for all times. This is the kind of reasoning one gets from folks who, from a place of ignorance, fear, and bigotry dare to presume that they can know the mind and intent of God for everyone; especially when they base their conclusions on one single fact.

It is precisely this kind of reasoning that gives rise to one of the Accusers' favorite slogans: "God created Adam and Eve, not Adam and Steve." They claim that this single scriptural fact necessarily implies that God did not intend for anyone, ever, to be LGBT; and absolutely would not *ever* create anyone that way.

Really? Seriously? It is incredibly arrogant of anyone to think that she or he can know the whole mind and complete intention of God for others. We often cannot accurately discern another *human being's* intent based on a single action. We do not have the capacity to read *each other's* minds. How dare they think that they can extrapolate the intent of God regarding human sexuality for all people, for all times, from the single fact that God made Adam and Eve, not Adam and Steve? I have no doubt that one day most people will view that reasoning with the same disdain that thinking people feel now when they read the above excerpt from *Loving*. In the meantime, I humbly offer my take on the matter.

If we accept a literal interpretation of the biblical creation stories, it seems a reasonable theory that one of God's intentions for Adam and Eve was that they would populate the Earth. That is not a deduction to which I leap based solely on the fact that God created them. According to Genesis 1:28, God told them to "be fruitful and multiply."

God decided that men would have sperm and women would have eggs. Granted, that decision did operate to ensure that babies would not be conceived without genetic contributions from both a male and a female. So back in the day, before in vitro fertilization and other reproductive technology, that meant that a man and a woman had to have sex in order for a child to be conceived. But, just as we must assume that our omniscient God knew that the boat was coming, we must also assume that God knew that reproductive technology would be here, eventually.

So it does not necessarily follow that God intended for every person who would ever be born, in the history of the world, to be heterosexual. That would imply that conceiving children is the only "God-approved" reason to have sex. And if that were true, then every sexually active infertile man or woman, including all post-menopausal women, would be operating outside of God's intent. For that matter, every heterosexual act engaged in with precautions to prevent conception would lie outside of God's intent; a belief held by some Accusers, but not all. The logic of the "Adam and Steve" argument fails in the hands of Accusers who do not condemn both married heterosexual couples who have sex with the intent of preventing conception and those who have sex without the possibility of conception.

So I wonder if there might be another reason why God created Adam and Eve, not Adam and Steve. Now, let's just think real hard: If we can, at least, agree that God's probable intent was to set into motion the human population of the planet *with the creation of only two people,* what *sense* would it have made for God to create two women or two men?

"PICKING AND CHOOSING"

I've spent a lot time prayerfully thinking about one of the Accusers' favorite arguments. It goes something like this: "Gay people who *call* themselves Christians want to pick and choose which parts of the Bible to obey and which parts to ignore. The whole Bible is the inerrant Word of God and it means *exactly* what it says. You don't get to pick and choose what scriptures you like and disobey the rest of them."

This line of thought rests on a foundational claim without which most of Accuser-type thinking could survive. Most Accusers claim that they take the whole Bible literally. They do not. Generally, I avoid "absolute"-type statements like the plague. This one, I am willing to make: Nobody takes the whole Bible literally. I do not care what they say. If they are not intentionally lying, then they are mistaken; the kind of mistake that evidences ignorance of much of the content of the Bible that they claim to take literally and live by.

There are many laws and prohibitions in the Bible that the Accusers disobey without a pang of guilt. Some are contained in the very same law codes as the ancient prohibitions upon which the Accusers rely. For now, I'll just mention a few of them.

Those law codes contain prohibitions against eating shellfish (Leviticus 11:10), cutting hair and trimming beards (Leviticus 19:27), touching or eating rabbit or pig (Leviticus 11:6-8), and wearing clothing made of different fabrics (Leviticus 19:19), among others that no fundamentalist Accusers I have ever heard of follow today.

I remember, during my search for peace with my sexual orientation, finding a lot of comfort from learning that those prohibitions were there. How is it, I wondered (and still do), that the Accusers can isolate Leviticus 18:22 from all of the laws and prohibitions around it and feel comfortable ignoring the rest of them, while insisting that 18:22 is a mandate for all people for all times? Why is that not the same kind of "picking and choosing" they accuse us of?

When I have asked Accusers that question, the answer I have gotten most often is something like, "The Old Testament is history. Obviously, some of what is in there does not apply today, because Jesus ushered in a new order. The New Testament tells Christians how to live, and we are supposed to take it literally and live by it."

Okay. Let's look at a couple of New Testament scriptures and see how the Accusers are doing with living by their literal meanings:

> I Corinthians 14:34: "Women should be silent in the churches. For they are not permitted to speak, but should be subordinate, as the law also says."

> I Corinthians 7:1: "Now concerning the matters about which you wrote: It is good for a man not to touch a woman."

Of course, if you ask me, the most authoritative voice in the Bible is that of Jesus, who according to Luke 14:26 said, "Whoever comes to me and does not hate father and mother, wife and children, brothers and sisters, yes, and even life itself, cannot be my disciple."

No need to belabor the point with a longer list of examples. This should be enough to show that the Accusers do not take all of the New Testament literally, either, as mandates to live by today. But they do not see themselves as "picking and choosing" what to obey. I am pretty sure that, if you show them these scriptures, most will have an explanation for why they are *not* to be taken literally. And that requires looking beyond the words of those verses to some broader context.

They will tell you that Paul was writing to the church at Corinth, in chapter 14; that the church was going through a lot of drama and some of the women were violating the customs of that time and place by speaking out and interrupting meetings. So Paul heard about it and wrote, to them, that the women should keep silent and subordinate, according to custom.

They will tell you that Paul considered himself to be called to a life of celibacy; and believed that was best for Christians. More important, when Paul wrote most of his letters in the Bible, he firmly believed that Jesus was coming back any day. So, while he spoke about marriage when called upon, he probably did not see life-long commitments like marriage as primary concerns. He thought it was all going to be over any minute.

And they will tell you that Jesus did not, literally, mean hate your parents, spouses, children, and siblings. He knew that the people to whom he was speaking would undergo harsh persecution. Some would be estranged from their families because of their conversion; and some would have to leave their homes and families and live in safe spaces. They will show you the verses immediately following that one, so you'll see that his point was that discipleship comes with a cost. It requires difficult choices, sometimes, and sacrifices. Most Accusers will tell you something like that. *None* will tell you that they, themselves, fail as disciples of Jesus Christ because they love their families.

My point is that the Accusers are *willing* to look at those scriptures in context, and to interpret them finding meanings other than the literal meanings of the words. So I can't help wondering—what is their investment in flatly rejecting all of the Bible scholarship and the science that support a different understanding of the "clobber passages" than the Accusers have had historically? Why do they insist that those passages must be taken literally as ethical mandates today?

WHAT THE BIBLE SAYS ABOUT HOMOSEXUALITY

A blank page could cover this topic. That is because the Bible says nothing about homosexuality. It is well-documented that the concept of sexual orientation, and the understanding that there is a spectrum of human sexuality, did not exist when the Bible was written. That does not mean that there were no homosexuals back then. It means that no one *understood* anyone to be homosexual. *So there is not one scripture that says one word about homosexuality, as we understand that word today*.

It is critical to a right understanding of the "clobber passages"—those used by the Accusers to beat us up—to distinguish homosexual acts or behavior from homosexual orientation. Anyone can commit a sexual act with anyone else, for any reason; including love, curiosity, drunken semi-consciousness, for money or other payment, as act of violence, or simply for fun and pleasure. People who are not gay can, and some have, engaged in homosexual behavior. People who are gay can, and some have, engaged in heterosexual behavior.

The "clobber passages" speak about homosexual acts in three specific contexts. A couple of references appear in the obsolete Israel-specific "law codes" discussed earlier (see "What is an Abomination, Anyway?"). The other references to same-gender sexual behavior are associated with the contexts of rape or ritualistic sexual practices in the worship of idol gods. Those are the sins to be found in those passages. There is nothing written in the Bible that addresses loving, non-exploitative relationships between persons of homosexual orientation. Some scholars posit that some well-known same-gender biblical characters appear to have been more than friends. Whether they were or not, they are not explicitly identified as same-gender-loving people; though if they were, it is noteworthy that they were written about with approval of their love and commitment to each other. In any event, I've never heard of their stories being used as "clobber passages;" probably because the Accusers assume they were just very close platonic friends.

The "clobber passages" that the Accusers do rely on all speak about instances of same-sex conduct by people who would have been presumed to be straight, because it was not understood that there is any other way for some people to be. The locations in which these scriptures are set were full of families consisting of men, women, and children. I know of no evidence that these were cities and countries where everyone was gay. So, if today's statistics are at all indicative of the percentage of gay people in those populations, *most of the people committing those acts probably were straight.* Therefore, these acts may have been "unnatural" for most of them. Like "abomination," "unnatural," used in this context, is a relative term. It does not mean the same thing for everyone.

These scenarios could not be farther removed from today's understanding that there are people whose natural sexual orientation is homosexual. They couldn't be farther removed from the relationships in which same-gender-loving Christians live today. Comparing the sex that was happening in these scriptures to loving, committed relationships between same-gender-loving people is like comparing the rape of a woman by a man to the love-making that occurs between a devoted husband and wife. Whatever the physical resemblances may be between those two acts, they are not the same acts. Neither can an orgy, perpetrated in a temple in honor of an idol god, be compared with loving sexual intimacy in the context of same-gender-loving relationships.

Jesus never said a word about same-sex relationships or homosexuality, and neither does the rest of the Bible. In any case, whenever people desecrate God's gift of sexual pleasure to commit rape or worship idols, I doubt very much that God's biggest problems with them have anything to do with their sexual orientation.

THE WORD IN THE WORDS

The presence of multiple literary genres in the Bible sends a clear signal that a sound understanding of it must have a basis that extends well beyond the literal meaning of its words. We understand, in all other contexts, that a poem, a letter by a specific person addressed to specific people, a historical account, an allegorical story, and a code of law cannot be read and used in the same ways. That also applies to the various literary genres present in the Bible. Not everything in there is meant to be a mandate for all people for all times.

In order for the Bible to serve its purpose in individual lives and for the Body of Christ and the world, it must be read and studied prayerfully and critically. The Bible is not God; and it is not my god. God, alone, is perfect and unfailing. God, alone, is capable of producing God's pure, unadulterated, and complete Word. Because God has chosen, among other ways, to partially reveal Godself through the products of collaboration with human beings, the results of those divine-human collaborations will necessarily reflect both the perfection of God and the limitations of human beings.

The Accusers have a hard time with that. Nonetheless, we all need to make our peace with the "human factor" in the Bible. No one claims that the whole Bible was written on tablets of stone by God, Godself. There is a human factor present; a big one. First, there was the initial handing down of much of its content from generation to generation by word-of-mouth. Anyone who has ever played the game where you whisper something to the person beside you, and it goes around the circle to see how close the original version of the statement is to what the last participant hears, knows how that usually works out. Then, there were those who wrote it down, the translations, the decisions about which documents would be included and which wouldn't, and the revisions. There are tons of scholarship about all of that; the details of which are beyond the scope of this essay. My point is that these are all human processes, not acts of God.

The refusal to acknowledge the presence of human influence and limitations in the final product that we know as the Bible today evidences a shortage of faith in the miracle of the Bible. The miracle is not that God dictated it, word-for-word to a group of ancient, divinely-chosen stenographers. The miracle of the Bible is that God provides the hugely diverse people of every generation of humanity with sacred, life-transforming, and perpetually relevant truths and principles that operate, for those who place ourselves under its authority, as "a lamp to [our] feet and a light to [our] path."

I encourage my congregation to read the Bible looking for "the Word in the words." When I am speaking, I always make sure to tell them that "Word," in that phrase, is capitalized; and that "words" is not. Then I refer them to the first chapter of John, verses one and fourteen: "In the beginning was the Word and the Word was with God and the Word was God. And the Word became flesh and lived among us, and we have seen his glory, the glory as of a father's only son, full of grace and truth." "Word," is capitalized there, too. Read together, those two verses tell us that the "Word" that John refers to is Jesus Christ. So we need not be afraid of the Bible, because 6-8 verses, out of more than 31,000, have been plucked out of their contexts and used as weapons to abuse and oppress us. We should read it, looking and listening for the Word in the words.

This means comparing what we read, in any given passage, to what the gospels tell us about Jesus and His gospel. He distilled all of the religious laws that preceded him down to, "Love God. Love neighbor." Jesus was all about relationships. He was about freedom and abundant life, not slavery to religious codes and establishments. He was the champion of the last, the least, and the lost of his day. It seems He preferred hanging out with them, too—not those who looked down on them, secure in their self-righteous superiority to them. He was about unconditional, all-inclusive love and grace, not condemnation.

Looking and listening for the Word in the words is about paying attention to whether what we read in the Bible—and what we are told that it means—is consistent with the Spirit of Christ. If not, then what we've been told that it means is wrong; and the church is *obliged* to question its long-standing interpretations.

For those who believe that God reveals the Word of God—the Spirit of Christ—*through* the words, there is no need to insist that the words, themselves, are "inerrant" and "infallible." We understand that the presence of the human factor in the words is no hindrance to the revelation of the inerrant and infallible Word of God through them. It requires a deeper, more mature, and more personal faith to believe that—to *experience that*—than to stubbornly pretend that the words are free of any influence except God's and are, therefore, "inerrant" and "infallible."

Even if we assume that the words of the Bible are "inerrant and infallible," it is irrefutable that the prevalent human understandings of the words, in any society, at any given time, are not. Throughout modern history God has spoken, in the hearts of those who would hear, to *correct* prevalent understandings of the Bible; to bring about political and social change in the interest of justice. The changes in most churches' policies and practices in matters of race, and gender are examples. Most churches have renounced interpretations of the Bible in which they formerly found justification for racism, segregation, slavery, and misogyny; and have embraced corrected understandings and interpretations that ultimately led them to denounce these discriminatory evils.

The Holy Spirit shows the church's errors to those who are less invested in their doctrines, dogmas, and in holding onto unearned privilege bestowed by the *status quo*, than in hearing God speak. The first few to hear God's correction, to be called to speak out against unjust systems and conditions that the church has participated in perpetuating, are the prophets of their generation who God calls and uses to correct the church. They are the founders of holy movements that slowly, but inevitably, spread throughout the Body of Christ and the world.

The Bible is not a "dead letter." The Bible is a collection of words through which the Living Word still speaks today. It is a tragic mistake to place higher authority in the words than in the Word revealed through them. The words are not God. The Word is.

S&M IN THE CHURCH

When I was in seminary, I was astounded to hear that some of my student colleagues were placed in internships at churches that specified requirements like, "must not be a minority," or "males only." I can only suppose that the rationale was that we students needed the experience we obtained through field placements, so the school had to go along with racist, sexist, and no-doubt, homophobic specifications.

I also had several painful conversations with some of my seminarian colleagues who acknowledged the racism and sexism in the churches from which they came to seminary, and to which they planned to return to serve upon graduation and ordination. Their reasoning: "I hope to go back to effect change from the inside." Or, "I grew up with those people. They are good, sincere people. They are just products of the time and environment in which they were formed." Or, "You can't just come out and tell people that they are wrong. You have to love and nurture them into seeing it for themselves."

The most heart-breaking of these conversations, though, were those I had with my closeted LGBT seminarian colleagues. They were training for pastoral ministry, committed to being ordained by churches that they knew would never ordain them if they came out as LGBT. I found these to be the most heart-breaking conversations of all because most of my colleagues who were willing to support and serve in racist churches were white; and most who were willing to serve in sexist churches were male. As sad as it was that they were committed to serving and supporting *churches* full of bigots, at least I could attribute their willingness to do that to their failure to take personally bigotry that was not directed toward them. But my LGBT colleagues made conscious choices to expend their precious God-given gifts of time, talent, and treasure to support and perpetuate churches that refuse to acknowledge *them* as full-fledged members of the Body of Christ—*while so many of their LGBT sisters and brothers are dying on the vine, spiritually, for want of hope and spiritual nurture.* That harvest is plentiful; but the laborers willing to do God's work there are far too few.

I could not help wondering whether my colleagues were really "called" to remain in those churches or simply lacked the courage and integrity to come out of their closets and live authentic lives. Some were in same-gender-loving relationships that they had to pretend were "just" friendships in their church environments. Is it just me? Or is there something horribly and sadly ironic about misrepresenting oneself in church, of all places; and about having to, in order to be welcomed at Christ's table?

I completely understand the overwhelming costs of coming out, as LGBT or an ally, in homophobic church environments. I understand that it is a struggle. I can see it being a process that takes time. I just do not see how people who are called and willing to devote their lives to serving the Lord can, ultimately, reconcile their knowledge that God loves *them*, and called *them*, with serving churches whose message to people *like* them is, "You are not fit or worthy to be fully included here." How do you, *in the name of all that is holy*, accept the welcome you are given by those churches knowing that it is conditioned upon your ability and willingness to pass for straight? How do you choose the inclusion that you purchase for yourself, by your silence, over speaking the truth; if not for the sake of your own integrity, then for the sake of playing no part in the damage that churches like that do to the millions of LGBT people for whom Christ died?

Lies of omission are real. We can tell ourselves, all we want to, that "it's nobody's business." If you know that if you were heterosexual, you would readily identify yourself as such in your church of choice—if only by showing up and introducing folks to your husband or wife—then a conscious, deliberate decision to do or say nothing that might reveal that you are LGBT is a lie of omission.

If you are resting on "it's nobody's business" because you know that being honest about it would get you kicked out, that is a lie of omission.

Sometimes staying in those churches is also downright masochistic; especially in churches where preachers get off on bashing LGBTs. I remember sitting in worship services listening to preachers carry on about homosexuality as an "abomination" and declaring that we are all demon-possessed reprobates who are going to Hell. Whenever that would happen, you could almost feel everyone's eyes darting toward whoever was in the room that we all *knew* was gay and living in a see-through closet. Most of the time, we did not have to turn our heads, because at least one or two were at the front of the church—in the pulpit or the choir, or seated at the piano or organ. Sometimes, we did not even have to divert our gaze from the preacher to whom we were listening.

Before I came out to myself, I always wondered how they felt; sitting there listening to the preacher rant about them that way. Sometimes, their carefully-contrived blank expressions would crack, just a little, revealing pain or humiliation; and I would feel sorry for them. Even then, it seemed incongruous for a minister of the gospel to find so much satisfaction in those rants. It struck me as just plain hateful and mean-spirited.

After God healed and integrated me enough for me to embrace my same-gender-loving self, I knew how they felt. Those vitriolic diatribes were caustic, scathing, and soul-searing assaults on the LGBT spirit. The preachers I heard do it seemed to take an orgasmic kind of pleasure in their fantasies of Hell bursting at the seams; packed to capacity with the burning and tortured souls of gay folk. The congregation would laugh, and encourage the preacher with shouts of "Amen!" and "Preach!" This, within sight and earshot of people who they knew were gay, and who embraced these congregations as family.

We, who are LGBT, must take responsibility for our choice to remain in those environments and have our spirits beaten up that way. We must seek healing from this mentality that bears a striking resemblance to "battered spouse syndrome." We must stop accepting the abuse. We must stop making excuses for them like, "Well, it only comes up every couple of months or so." Or, "They don't know any better. Most of them just aren't educated enough to understand homosexuality, and that it's not a choice." Or, "This is the only hurtful thing that they do or say. Everything else about this church is just exactly what I believe in and need. So the good outweighs the bad." Even, "My family is there. My friends are there. Everyone I love and everyone who loves me is there. I couldn't bear to lose them."

I know, I know, *I know* how hard that is to face. But the simple truth is that if you have to be abused to be accepted *anywhere*, that is a place you don't need to be. And anyone who will not love you if they know whatever is true about you, does not love *you* now. They "love" the person they think you are; or can pretend they think you are, as long as you remain silent about your gayness, sit through the abuse, and remain complicit in your own oppression, and that of every other LGBT person who enters that place.

We must trust that those in our homophobic Accuser-churches who really do love us will continue to, even if they do not understand or approve. Those relationships may not be the same. Or it may take time, and hard work, for those relationships to heal to whatever extent they will. But those who really love you will still love you. They will eventually realize that nothing has changed except a single fact that they now know about you. Sometimes, not even that. So often, they eventually admit that they always knew. In any case, those who are willing to be honest will have to admit that you have not changed because of what you have just acknowledged. It has been true, and a part of you, all the time.

We must trust that, once we commit to living in truth and integrity, God will direct our paths to churches, friendships, and relationships where we will be loved for who we are.

Those, who are not LGBT, bear responsibility for the pain they inflict or support by their participation or passivity in Accuser-church gay-bashing. You cannot hide behind your claims to "love the sinner, hate the sin." You are not abusing the "sin." The "sin" does not bear the horrific emotional and spiritual scars you inflict. The "sin" does not go home from your churches, after one of your preachers has worked you all up into a homophobic hate-fest, filled with self-loathing and terror over the prospect of losing its soul. The "sin" doesn't agonize over what it cannot change. The "sin" is not vulnerable to believing that it has been forsaken by God because God is not changing it either. Your "hating the sin" is not hurting the "sin." We are human beings, with souls, that you are judging, condemning, and sentencing to a Hell that you neither own nor control. We are human beings—including thousands of *teen-agers*—who have been driven to hopelessness and self-destructive behavior, including suicide, by your brand of "love."

Personally, I'd prefer that you not love me, if you don't have the capacity to do better at it than that. But I know that being faithful to the *Spirit* of Christ would compel and help you to do better; because, as a Christian and a human being, I hate *your* sin. I hate the self-righteous presumptuousness that leads you to believe that you have the information or the right to judge another person's standing before God. I hate the stiff-necked disobedience that you commit every time you defy those scriptures that clearly instruct us not to judge one another. (Why don't you take *those* literally?) I hate the abject cruelty that many of you display as you take delight in speaking the words, "They are going to Hell!" I hate your willful, ongoing ignorance as you simply refuse to accept, often refuse to even read or hear, the huge body of information, from every credible scientific, social, and biblical academy that refutes the notion that homosexuality is a choice and a sin. I hate the destruction that you wreak on families—your own, as you turn your backs on your LGBT children, siblings, and parents; and ours, as you tirelessly campaign and vote to deny us human rights and legal privileges that you have long taken for granted. I hate that, hiding behind "hating the sin" you talk to and about us, and behave toward us, *in ways that are indistinguishable on every level from hating us*. And I hate, most of all, that you do it all in the name of Jesus.

I hate your sin. But I would not speak a word or lift a finger to inflict the kind of pain and damage on you that you have inflicted on us; because that would be inconsistent with my understanding of what it means to be a Christian. You will never hear me judge your standing before God, or say that you are going to Hell for your sins that I see or your sins that I don't see; because that would be inconsistent with my faith in what Jesus did for ***whosoever*** believes in him.

Not everyone in Accuser-churches, with official homophobic theology, policies and practices is, in fact, homophobic. That's the good news. Unfortunately, those who are not do their share of damage, too, by their passive support of churches that perpetuate exclusion that they know to be wrong. For many, it is a classic case of, "when good people do nothing." Except they do not exactly do nothing. They support these bastions of abusive bigotry by their presence, service, finances, and silence. In order for the church, as the Body of Christ, to be faithful to the Spirit of Christ, it is necessary to refuse to adhere to policies and practices that implicitly bestow unearned privilege on some by explicitly excluding, abusing, or marginalizing others. It is necessary for the "good people" who benefit from the privilege to renounce it. During the various stages of struggle for racial civil rights, somebody had to have the guts to say, to their good, God-fearing, slave-buying-and-selling, Jim-Crow-perpetrating, exclusive-country-club-patronizing families, churches, peers and neighbors, "The ways that we have always thought; the systems that we have always supported; and our use of a few isolated Bible verses to justify our injustice and oppression of these people is *wrong*." Somebody—on the inside—had to be willing to risk being thrown out for speaking up and saying, "It is a slap in the face of everything that Jesus taught and demonstrated by his life and ministry for the church—of all people, places, and institutions—to continue to operate like an exclusive club, and I will not support, or be a part of, any church whose official theology and policy perpetrate that atrocity, in the name of Jesus Christ."

It is time for all who "get" Jesus; who understand His gospel of liberation from letter of the law under which we *all* fall short, to stop supporting churches whose official theology and policy perpetuate the judgment, exclusion or limited inclusion of any sub-set of the full and complete spectrum of humanity for which Christ died. Because, Good People, if the LGBTs among you are the masochists in this drama, what does that make the Accusers and those who support them?

The Accuser Within

Many LGBT Christians who have been indoctrinated with homophobic messages and Bible abuse have some degree of internalized homophobia. The condemning messages play over and over in our minds like "old tapes;" haunting and taunting us as we take the arduous journey toward wholeness—integration of all aspects of ourselves; our spirituality and sexuality peacefully co-existing within us; deliverance from our fear of God's punishment for being who we are. The effects of our internalized homophobia are profound and pervasive. Some are obvious and some are so subtle we may not recognize them ourselves until they are pointed out to us.

Some of us spend huge chunks of our lives battling depression that has its source in our deep-seated belief that we are "bad." When bad things happen in our lives, we have a nagging suspicion that it is God's punishment for being same-gender-loving people, even though we know those same things happen to straight people every day. When our intimate relationships crumble, we often do not attribute that to any of the many factors that give rise to a fifty-percent divorce rate among heterosexuals. In our heart of hearts, we believe that our relationships fail because they were wrong, in the first place; that God did not (would not) ordain our relationships, and did not (would never) bless them. If we are completely honest, some would have to admit to a feeling of relief, with every break-up, that the end of our intimate relationships restores our relatively "safe" status as "non-practicing" homosexuals; at least, for as long as we remain celibate. We find ways to sabotage our own happiness and success because, deep down inside, we believe we are undeserving of either.

For us to be happy, somehow, compounds the "sin" of being gay. Our internalized homophobia tells us it is a double slap in God's face to be wrong *and* to have the nerve to be happy. And so whatever pain, grief, illness, financial challenges, and misery we suffer seems, somehow, only fitting. To be free from guilt and shame, we fear, would seal our fate as reprobates.

Reprobates are people who have no regard for God. They do not care about right and wrong. Pleasing God is among the least of their concerns. Each of us knows, in our own heart, whether that is true of us. It is not true of any of the hundreds of LGBT Christians I know, and to whom I have ministered. I doubt it is true of anyone who would read this book. If you love God, you are not a reprobate. If the thought that God may not love you, or may be disappointed in you, grieves you, you are not a reprobate. *If, contrary to everything you were taught, you know that the Spirit of God dwells within you; that the hand of God rests upon you, and that God moves and works in you, through you, and on your behalf, you are NOT a reprobate.* If you could believe that God created and loves you, as the LGBT person you are, and if believing that would transform your life and restore your joy in the Lord, you are not a reprobate. And if, upon being reconciled and restored, your heart's deepest desire would be to discern and do the will of God, for the glory of God, you are not a reprobate. You are not even close. Reprobates do not care whether they are reprobates or not.

> *We do not need to suffer the torment of the Accuser within to keep us on the right side of the line between redeemable and reprobate. We are redeemed already and forever, by the saving work of Jesus Christ.*

The Accuser within can be divested of his/her/their power over us. That is, itself, a progressive healing process that, for most of us, takes some time and conscious effort. But it can be done, by learning to distinguish the voice of the Accuser within from the voice of the Spirit of God. The Accuser speaks via "old tapes," which are nothing more than memories of things we heard and were taught in our Accuser homes, churches, schools, and other Accuser environments. The Accuser says the same things over and over again: "It's an abomination." "You're going to Hell." "You are a pervert." "You have a demon." "It's unnatural." "It's a sin." "You know you're wrong." And the beat goes on . . .

We must not confuse our memory of things spoken by human beings yesterday, with the voice of God speaking to us today. When the Spirit of the Lord speaks within us, it's live, not Memorex. There are no old-tape repetitions of the same stale accusatory phrases. God speaks to us in the moment, with a fresh and refreshing Word every time.

When the Accuser within speaks, it is in the voice(s) of people we have known. Listen carefully, next time. Identify the voice(s) of your Accuser within. Do not try to ignore the old tapes. That will never silence them. Listen to what they say and how they say it, and let yourself recognize whose voices they are. Because when you do, you will realize that the voice(s) of your Accuser within is not that of God. You will recognize the voice(s) of your childhood priest or pastor, or your grandmother, or your parents, or whoever imprinted you with their condemning, homophobic theology and recorded those old tapes that re-play in your mind now. Whoever they are, you will realize that they are *human beings* to whom you have surrendered your power to claim your place in the Body of Christ as one who believes in him. John 1:11-12—"He came unto his own, and his own received him not. But as many as received him, to them gave he power to become the [children] of God, even to them that believe on his name." Any power that was ours to surrender is ours to take back; especially power given to us by God, in the person of Jesus Christ. We never had God's permission to give it away. We do not need the Accusers' permission to take it back.

It is imperative to learn to talk back to the Accuser within. When Jesus was led into the wilderness to be tempted by Satan, Jesus talked back to Satan straight from the scripture. And it, eventually, shut Satan up and Satan departed from Jesus. When the old tapes start playing, we must talk back to our Accuser within the same way:

Accuser: "It's an abomination!"

Answer: "You shall love the Lord your God with all your heart, and with all your soul, and with all your mind." This is the greatest and first commandment. And a second is like it: "You shall love your neighbour as yourself." On these two commandments hang all the law and the prophets." (Matthew 22:37-40)

Accuser: "You are demon possessed!"

Answer: "By this you know the Spirit of God: every spirit that confesses that Jesus Christ has come in the flesh is from God . . ." (1 John 4:2)

Accuser: "You are going to Hell!"

Answer: "For God so loved the world that he gave his only begotten Son, so that ***whosoever*** believeth in him should not perish but have eternal life." (John 3:16)

Accuser: "God hates homosexuals, bisexuals and transgendered persons!"

Answer: "God is love." (1 John 4:8b)

Accuser: "You are a pervert!"

Answer: "For we are what he has made us, created in Christ Jesus for good works, which God prepared beforehand to be our way of life." (Ephesians 2:10)

Accuser: "You have no right to call yourself a Christian!"

Answer: "Who are you to pass judgment on servants of another? It is before their own lord that they stand or fall. And they will be upheld, for the Lord is able to make them stand." (Romans 14:4)

Accuser: "You are living in sin!"

Answer: "For by ***grace*** you have been saved through ***faith***, and this is not your own doing; it is the gift of God—not the result of works, so that no one may boast." (Ephesians 2:8-9)

Accuser: "You are a reprobate, beyond redemption!"

Answer: "For I am persuaded, that neither death, nor life, nor angels, nor principalities, nor powers, nor things present, nor things to come, nor height, nor depth, nor any other creature, shall be able to separate us from the love of God, which is in Christ Jesus our Lord." (Romans 8:38-39)

Speaking of Jesus, the better we get to know him, the easier it is to distinguish his voice from those of our Accusers. He is the Word in the words of the Bible; and his Spirit is still speaking today.

Most of us have known, at least, a few people so well that, even after they pass away, we can "hear" them speak to us in our minds. My father passed away in 1995; and my mother exactly twelve weeks ago, as of the date of this writing. In almost any situation, I can make a well-educated guess of what advice they would give me. When we know people well, we know what sounds like them and what does not. When others report that someone we know supposedly said this or that, we can often immediately respond with, "That sounds just like her!" Or with, "He would never say that. That doesn't even sound like him."

We can get to know Jesus so well, by studying his life, teachings, and ministry, and through the Holy Spirit, that when we hear hateful, condemning rhetoric, purportedly spewed forth in his name, we will know that does not even sound like him. It is completely inconsistent with how he lived and what he taught. It is hate speech; the language of injustice. And he was all about justice for all—not in the modern legal sense in which "justice" is equated with punishment for the guilty and acquittal for the innocent. If that were the case, we would all be without hope, for we all have sinned and come short of the glory of God. Jesus was about social justice—the elimination of systems of privilege and powerlessness; have and have-nots; insiders and outsiders. How profoundly ironic it is that the church has, by and large, become such a system!

Jesus said that sheep know the voice of their shepherd. He is our Shepherd. His voice, and his words, are not those of the Accusers within or around us. The more we learn of him, the easier it is to immediately distinguish his voice from those old tapes playing in our minds. We hear them less and less frequently; and at those times when we do, we are well-armed and ready to answer.

THE GOD THAT I KNOW

According to the Book of Joshua, when the Israelites were preparing to conquer the city of Jericho, Joshua passed on instructions to them from God that included the following:

> The city and all that is in it shall be devoted to the LORD for destruction. Only Rahab the prostitute and all who are with her in her house shall live, because she hid the messengers we sent. As for you, keep away from the things devoted to destruction, so as not to covet and take any of the devoted things and make the camp of Israel an object for destruction, bringing trouble upon it. Joshua 6:17-18

The instructions were given, and one of the people, Achan, disobeyed them. He took some of the spoils that were devoted to destruction for himself. God got mad; not only at Achan, but at all of Israel and forsook them during their next battle against the Amorites. When Joshua asked God why God had forsaken them God said:

> Stand up! Why have you fallen upon your face? Israel has sinned; they have transgressed my covenant that I imposed on them. They have taken some of the devoted things; they have stolen, they have acted deceitfully, and they have put them among their own belongings. Therefore the Israelites are unable to stand before their enemies; they turn their backs to their enemies, because they have become a thing

> devoted for destruction themselves. I will be with you no more, unless you destroy the devoted things from among you. Proceed to sanctify the people, and say, "Sanctify yourselves for tomorrow; for thus says the LORD, the God of Israel, 'There are devoted things among you, O Israel; you will be unable to stand before your enemies until you take away the devoted things from among you.' In the morning therefore you shall come forward tribe by tribe. The tribe that the LORD takes shall come near by clans, the clan that the LORD takes shall come near by households, and the household that the LORD takes shall come near one by one. And the one who is taken as having the devoted things shall be burned with fire, together with all that he has, for having transgressed the covenant of the LORD, and for having done an outrageous thing in Israel." Joshua 7:10-15

Joshua followed these instructions from God, and eventually Achan confessed that he had stolen some of the devoted spoils. God's instructions were carried out:

> So Joshua sent messengers, and they ran to the tent; and there it was, hidden in his tent with the silver underneath. They took them out of the tent and brought them to Joshua and all the Israelites; and they spread them out before the LORD. Then Joshua and all Israel with him took Achan son of Zerah, with the silver, the mantle, and the bar of gold, with his sons and daughters, with his oxen, donkeys, and sheep, and his tent and all that he had; and they brought them up to the Valley of Achor. Joshua said, 'Why did you bring trouble on us? The LORD is bringing trouble on you today.' And all Israel stoned him to death; they burned them with fire, cast stones on them, and raised over him a great heap of stones that remains to this day. Then the LORD turned from his burning anger. Therefore that place to this day is called the Valley of Achor. Joshua 7:22-28

Most Accusers still serve this God. It is as if they "missed the memo" that we call the Gospel. They apparently still think of God as One who lays down rules, gives instructions, gets furious with us and forsakes us when we disobey, and is not mollified until we have been severely punished.

That is not the God I know. The God I know recognized that we all would sin and fall short of God's glory. Romans 6:23 does not say, "For the wages of sin is death, but the reward for theological and ecclesiastical conformity is eternal life." It says, "For the wages of sin is death, but the gift of God is eternal life." The God I know loved the world, as in everyone, so much that God *replaced* the wages of sin with the *gift* of eternal life. I accept my salvation as a gift of God, made available to all of us by grace, through faith.

Contrary to the reasoning of the Accusers, embracing the freedom that is ours under the New Covenant of the Gospel of Jesus Christ is not a manifestation of licentiousness. It is pure and complete *faith* in God's grace, not abuse of it. It is truly understanding that no one is going to Heaven because he or she has earned it. And no one is going to Hell because of failure to earn entry into Heaven.

Having this understanding does not automatically lead to licentiousness. For those who believe the pure, unembellished, gospel of Jesus Christ, as He proclaimed it before there was any such thing as a church, it leads to profound gratitude to God for what God has done for us. It leads to the desire to live holy lives; which if that means anything, means living honestly and in integrity. It is irrelevant that a lot of people, most of whom claim to have no experience of anything other than heterosexual orientation or urges, presume to pronounce that our gayness is a choice. We who never made such a choice know that we did not. We know that we are what God has made us, created in Christ Jesus, for good works which God prepared beforehand to be our way of life. (Ephesians 2:10) This is what we know. And when, in spite of all of the chatter of the Accusers, the Holy Spirit bears witness to that truth in us, abusing God's grace is not something we ever want to do.

If the Accusers have done us one favor, they have ensured that we are far less likely than they are to see ourselves as worthy of God's grace in our own right. If anything, we rely on the grace of God in a way that is mutually exclusive with self-righteousness;

because, if I am to be completely honest, some of us never achieve complete immunity to the spiritual violence the Accusers inflict on us. Even among those who do, for many it is a long process of many years during which the harsh judgmental criticism of a sibling, or the pleading of a grandmother who just doesn't get it to "repent" and change, or the coldness and distance we feel during the occasional visit to the churches that we believed would be our life-long spiritual homes and extended families, or yet another news item showing that homophobia is alive and well in the society in which we live—any of those things, and many others, can trigger our learned internalized homophobia and set us back for a minute.

But God is faithful to minister to us and remind us that we, too, are God's beloved children and members of the Body of Christ. God reminds us, in response to our pain and our unique need for reassurance, that nobody is going to Heaven for being straight and no one will be excluded there for being LGBT. God is faithful in allowing us to have our own experience of God's work of grace in our lives. To paraphrase a beloved hymn, God walks with us; God talks with us; God tells us we are God's own. We live with a deep consciousness that our hope is built on nothing less than Jesus' blood and *His* righteousness, not our own. For us to finally get to that spiritual posture, in spite of everything the Accusers throw at us, gives rise to gratitude to God so profound that it is a far greater motivation to live and work for God, and to be the best people we can be, than the fear of Hell has ever been.

BY THEIR FRUIT YOU SHALL KNOW THEM

Many LGBT Christians find it hard to decide to leave Accuser-churches that abuse us because they are not sure that "open and affirming" churches are "real" churches led by "real" anointed spiritual leaders. We are already terrified by what we have heard about ourselves from our Accusers. The last thing we want to do is place ourselves under the pastoral care of ministers who the Accusers call "false prophets;" who, in complete contradiction to the dogma of the churches in which we were raised, actually affirm us as the beloved children of God that we are.

After I learned about the existence of "open and affirming" churches, it took a long time for me to find the courage to seriously consider going to one. Eventually, I read the book, *Our Bodies, Ourselves*, in which there were chapters about sexuality and spirituality. I do not remember which edition or which chapter it was; only that somewhere in that book I read something that informed me that there are people in this world who do not see being homosexual as being automatically antithetical to being a Christian. I was in my thirties; and I did not know that such people existed.

Something that I read led me to write to the publisher. I poured out the pain, fear, and confusion in my heart as I tried to reconcile what I knew about my relationship with God with what I had been taught about homosexuality. And I asked if they could refer me to a gay-affirmative Christian counselor or anyone who could help me.

I received a letter informing me that my letter had been forwarded to St. John's Metropolitan Community Church ("MCC") in Raleigh, NC; and that I should hear from someone there soon. Within a few days, I received a telephone call from a minister there. She invited me to church and offered to pick me up and take me there. I was impressed that she would do that for a total stranger. I owe her an eternal debt for that act of kindness, because I do not know if, or how long it would have taken, for me to come up with the courage to go on my own.

That was the beginning of my relationship with MCC; and of my journey toward reconciliation with the institutional church. I was re-educated, nurtured, and set on a course of progressive healing in MCC. The anointing that God placed upon me was recognized and the exercise of the gifts God gave me was welcomed and encouraged there. I learned about the inextricable connection between being a disciple of Jesus Christ and being a warrior for social justice there. I was inspired, by the founder, pastors and leaders of that Denomination, to say "yes" to my own call to Christian ministry, with the understanding that I was, by that same act, saying "no" to remaining silent about my identity as a Christian and a lesbian; and to remaining unresponsive to the Accusers' spiritual torment of LGBT children of God. I have been a member of three MCC's since that first visit to St. John's; currently as the pastor of MCC-New Haven, CT.

In the last few years, MCC has been in partnership with The Fellowship; a network of mostly African-American, Pentecostal affirming churches and pastors. The Rev. Dr. Yvette Flunder is the founder and Presiding Bishop of that organization. My association with The Fellowship returned to me the gift of freedom to re-claim every good thing associated with the Pentecostal background from which I came to MCC. I no longer feel unworthy of the outpouring of the Holy Spirit in worship. I understand that it was never about *my* worthiness, anyway. It is, has always been, and will always be a gift of grace imparted by God, according to God's own will. I can get my praise on, again, in liberty and with gratitude! Bishop Flunder, along with her life partner, Mother Shirley Miller, have quickly risen to the "top tier" of my spiritual inspirations, along with Rev. Elder Troy Perry, the founder of the Metropolitan Community Churches; Rev. Elder Nancy Wilson, our current Moderator; and other leaders of both organizations.

The Accusers call trailblazing spiritual leaders like these, and the pastors and ministers who they nurture into stepping fully into our callings, "false prophets." They say we are "condoning sin," and leading people along a path that leads straight to Hell. Why we do this depends on which Accuser you ask. Some say we need to justify our own "sinful" sexual practices. Others say we have "sold out to the world" or to "today's society," and have sacrificed faithfulness to scripture on the altar of political correctness. Some say that we are demon possessed; or that we have been given over to reprobate minds. They say we are "false prophets and a danger to the souls of those who trust our leadership and our message of God's radically inclusive and unconditional love manifested in the person of Jesus Christ.

I cannot speak for, or about, every LGBT or LGBT-affirming minister. My guess is that there some among us with questionable motives and ethics as surely as, God knows, there are among "mainstream" and Accuser ministers, priests, and pastors. I can only echo the scripture, and suggest looking at our fruits. "Every good tree bears good fruit, but the bad tree bears bad fruit." (Matthew 7:17)

Looking at a spiritual leader's fruit is not the same thing as looking at the spiritual leader. There are none among us—gay, straight, affirming, or Accuser—who is perfect. If you look at *us*, you are going to find something to judge and interpret to mean that we are unworthy of our call and anointing. Every honest spiritual leader will tell you that.

A spiritual leader's fruit has nothing to do with whether the leader conforms to requirements that an institutional church seeks to impose upon him or her. *A spiritual leader's fruit is comprised of the spiritual impact of his or her ministry upon those to whom she or he ministers, and in the ways that impact manifests itself in the world.*

What is the spiritual impact of preaching and teaching that God hates an entire population of people based solely on their sexual orientation, gender identity, or gender expression? What is the spiritual impact on those people? What is the spiritual impact of encouraging congregations to believe that they are "better," more "worthy," more "righteous," because their sexual orientation, gender identity, and gender expression conform to that of the majority?

What is the "ripple effect" of that kind of preaching and teaching out in the world?

In September of 2010, at least six gay teenagers in the U.S. committed suicide as a result of bullying and emotional torture by their peers. I do not know whether these particular young people had families and churches, or other religious communities, who would have been sources of support for them; but I know that far too many do not. What factors create an environment in which some people—some who identify themselves as Christians—feel fully justified in mentally, emotionally, and physically abusing LGBT's? Accuser pastors, priests, popes, and televangelists must take some responsibility for contributing to the atmospheric hostility toward LGBT's that manifests itself in countless tragedies. *They are telling millions of people, within their collective international sphere of influence, that even God despises us!* Why *wouldn't* those who believe them feel fully justified in doing the same? Why wouldn't those, who are so inclined, see inflicting violence upon us as justified; even as pleasing to God? Accuser-pastors are feeding their fear, and contributing to the misinformation about who we are in relation to God. From their pulpits, they take their sacred duty to proclaim the "good news" of the gospel as opportunities to rant about us and call us everything but children of God. They pluck a handful of scripture verses out of context and perpetuate the erroneous belief that these scriptures refer, and apply, to loving relationships between same-gender-loving people of homosexual orientation, as we understand those concepts today. How surprised should they be when some of their own children feel justified in torturing LGBT kids; and when some LGBT children would rather die than to grow up, if they must do so in the environments the Accusers create, to be the people they feel destined to be? *By their fruit,* you shall know them.

I am blessed to witness, and participate in, a ministry movement that preaches and teaches God's radically inclusive, unconditional love for all of humanity. The spiritual leaders I know and follow testify of deep personal relationship with God; some from their early childhood. Many grew up, were nurtured and formed in Accuser churches. But their realization that they are homosexual forced them to leave those churches if they were to live honestly and in integrity.

Either that, or the Accuser churches, themselves, kicked them out when they came out; as if the church of the Lord Jesus Christ is some kind of country club where one must meet certain criteria to be an "insider" and everyone else is an "outsider." Well, they can kick an LGBT out of a local church, but no one can amputate us from the Body of Christ. We are among those for whom Christ died, and as long as we *believe* that, no one is authorized to limit the reach of the "whosoever" in John 3:16.

This is a message of hope, healing, and reconciliation for millions of people. The spiritual leaders that I know and follow have exhibited tremendous courage in speaking truth to those in power in the "mainstream" church. Their ministries have, literally, saved countless lives. The LGBT folks to whom they minister have had their belief in God's love for them restored. They have shaken off their "grave clothes" of despair and have been resurrected into new life in Jesus Christ. They have become new creatures—not straight creatures, *new* creatures—committed to living by those principles that Jesus *did* talk about, rather than feeling condemned by something he never mentioned at all. "Love God with all your heart and love your neighbor as yourself" are the primary precepts that govern their lives; and that transforms their lives in ways so wonderful that they live in loving gratitude and joy unspeakable and full of glory. They lay aside the real sins and weights that they took on in a mind-set of hopeless and resignation that they were going to Hell, anyway, so there was no need to try to live righteous lives. They are asking and exploring ethical questions that they once believed were moot for them; and changing their ways of relating to others to conform to their new understanding that to be gay is to be gay and to be Christian is to be Christian, and the two are not mutually exclusive. The former is not a choice; the latter is. And it is a choice available to them. Many are healed of their addictions, and abandon their conscious or unconscious efforts to commit suicide via self-destructive behaviors that reflected their deep self-hatred and despair. They are, instead, committing time, talent, and treasure toward moving us all closer to the full realization of the reign of God—a world in which justice for all will be more than a catchy phrase at the end of the pledge of allegiance.

The ministries of LGBT-affirming spiritual leaders are producing hopeful, joyful, grateful, God-and-neighbor loving, progressively healthier citizens of their communities, workplaces, schools, and society; people who are living to live again in the immediate presence of the Lord and Savior of us all. *By their fruits*, you shall know them.

When I was working through my coming out, there was no Internet to facilitate finding an open and affirming church. Thank God, it is not as difficult to find one now; both because of the Internet and because there are more of them to be found. It is no different than searching for any other kind of church. Not every one will be for everybody. One has to find the right "fit" with an open and affirming church that meets one's needs. But there are plenty of churches, like MCC's and those affiliated with The Fellowship, among others, where LGBT Christians and all Christians, for that matter, can be ministered to by called, anointed men and women of God. The fact that they affirm us, as the full-fledged beloved children of God that we are, does not make them "false prophets." In the current, temporarily Accuser-dominated church-world, it just makes them prophets; among the first to see and declare what everyone will see eventually.

AN OPEN LETTER TO THE ACCUSERS

I do not address you to argue about the meaning of the handful of scriptures you use against us. Nor will I take this opportunity to discuss the science that unanimously refutes the notion that homosexuality is an illness or indicative of demonic occupation. There is just too much information available to you, already, for me to imagine that hearing it from me would have any more effect than hearing it from experts in those disciplines.

I am appealing to your desire to do the right thing; to live right; to obey God's word. Many of you claim to take the Bible literally. If that is the case, please, just entertain a few questions from me; not to answer me, but to answer them for yourselves.

What is your understanding of the literal meaning of the following scriptures?

> "For God so loved the world that he gave his only begotten Son that **whosoever believeth in him** should not perish, but have everlasting life." (John 3:16)

> "That if thou shalt **confess with thy mouth** the Lord Jesus, and shalt **believe in thine heart that God hath raised him from the dead,** thou **shalt** be saved." (Romans 10:9)

> "For by ***grace*** you have been saved through ***faith***, and this is not your own doing; it is the **gift** of God—not the result of works, so that no one may boast." (Ephesians 2:8-9)

Let's pretend, just for a moment, that you are not allowed to embellish these scriptures, to add to them or subtract from them, or to super-impose any belief you have about what it means to "live right," upon them. According to their plain literal meaning, where would you find a basis for treating LGBT Christians as any less Christian than you are?

The gospel of Jesus Christ states one requirement for salvation. Everything else is about ethics. One of your errors has been to confuse the scriptural content of the *gospel* with scriptural content about *ethics*. In other words, we all are Christians by virtue of our faith. I do not suggest that the way any of us live and behave is unimportant. This is not an assertion that "anything goes." It is an assertion that it is not up to you to determine what "goes" for me; anymore than it is up to you to determine where I am going when I die. The questions about what Christians should or should not do; what is "right" and what is "sin"—those are *ethical* questions about which we should be able to agree to disagree without passing judgment on the sincerity of each other's *faith* or on each other's worthiness to be embraced by our respective churches *as believers in Christ;* as members of the Body of *Christ*.

There are thousands of Christian denominations in the world. No doubt most of them are small and little-known off-shoots of larger denominations. So let's just look at a few of the major ones in the United States. Some say, "Baptize in the name of the Father, Son, and Holy Ghost" while others say, "Baptize in the name of Jesus." Some say, "Sunday is the Sabbath" while others say, "Saturday is the Sabbath." Some strictly prohibit any consumption of alcoholic beverages, while others serve wine for their Communion and cocktails at their Christmas parties. Some baptize their infants, while others honor no baptism that is not a believer's own choice after accepting the Lord as Savior. Some still will not ordain women, while others who formerly would not have come around to doing so. Some are racially segregated and determined to remain so, while most—after years of debate and many race-based church splits—eventually came around to renouncing racial exclusion and separatism as an acceptable ethic for a Christian church. *And all of them can point to scriptures the literal meanings of which support their own position.*

None of these ethical issues and practices has anything to do with the single requirement for salvation—faith in the Lord Jesus Christ. We all should be very careful not to add agreement with, and adherence to, our ethical beliefs to that requirement. Those who do Trinitarian baptism believe in Jesus Christ. Those who do "Jesus only" baptism believe in Jesus Christ. Those who don't touch wine, and those who serve it at the Lord's table, believe in Jesus Christ. As an African-American, female, same-gender-loving woman, I am willing to posit that there are racists, sexists, homophobes, and homo-abusers who sincerely believe in Jesus Christ. I just don't think they know him very well.

According to scripture, we are all members of the Body of Christ by virtue of our faith in him. We must distinguish the gospel of Jesus Christ—salvation by grace through faith—from the many, varied, and often conflicting codes of ethics that have evolved and been codified in the doctrine, dogma, and criteria for inclusion of our churches. The failure to make that distinction results in a perversion of the gospel. It renders what is clearly meant to be a free gift of *God,* and available to all, a mere status that *churches* presume to bestow or revoke based on their own ethical codes and criteria.

A church's failure to distinguish the singular requirement for salvation from its own ethical codes also results in the perversion of that church, itself. If you are preaching and practicing the exclusion of LGBT's from your church, simply because we are LGBT, you are perverting what was meant to be a house of prayer for all people into an exclusive club of folks who must meet criteria *you* have set to be welcomed, embraced, and valued equally.

Does it really never trouble you that you do that? Do you really believe that that is what the Church is meant to be? Have you ever asked yourself what if you're wrong about us? What if "whosoever" really does mean *who-so-ever*? What would it be like, for you, if you would have to answer for the souls that you rejected, ejected, wounded, and alienated from the church? What if Jesus would ask you, "Did you not read John 3:16; or did you simply refuse to accept that it means 'whosoever'?" What would you say? If He would ask you, "Did the Bible not tell you that it is about grace and faith, not works?" How would you respond to that?

More important, how would you expect Jesus to respond to you? Imagine, just for a moment, that you got it wrong. Imagine that, on the other side of the grave, you find out that "whosoever" really does mean who-so-ever; and "do not judge" really does mean "do NOT judge." What if you find out that it's true that, in Christ, there is neither male nor female; so as far as God is concerned, the "rightness" or "wrongness" of intimate relationships has nothing to do with physical bodies, gender or laws; and everything to do with the spirit in which we engage in them? Imagine that you are in that place where all things pertaining to flesh have passed out of the picture; and only souls live in the immediate presence of the Lord. Imagine that, once your spiritual vision is no longer impeded by your eyes, you see all of the injury you inflicted on every LGBT soul that you judged, marginalized, and excluded from your churches; on every child you disowned; every family member you ostracized. Do you really believe that God—who is Love—would cast your soul into Hell, because you made a theological mistake? Or would our loving God, who knows your heart, know that you did your best to discern and do God's will; look at you—*and* your errors *and* your hurtful, judgmental sins against LGBT believers in Christ—through the blood of God's Son and keep God's promise to you that you have eternal life, because you believed in Him?

What do you do with scriptures like, "Who are you to pass judgment on servants of another? It is before their own lord that they stand or fall. And they will be upheld, for the Lord is able to make them stand." (Romans 14:4) If you are so committed to literal interpretation of scripture, what hermeneutical maneuvering gets you around the plain meaning of:

> "Do not judge, so that you may not be judged." (Matthew 7:1);

> "Do not judge, and you will not be judged; do not condemn, and you will not be condemned. Forgive, and you will be forgiven . . ." (Luke 6:37);

"The Father judges no one but has given all judgement to the Son, so that all may honour the Son just as they honour the Father. Anyone who does not honour the Son does not honour the Father who sent him. Very truly, I tell you, *anyone who hears my word and believes him who sent me has eternal life, and does not come under judgement, but has passed from death to life*." (John 5:22-24, emphasis added). Jesus said that. How do you justify paying more attention to *any* other voice in the Bible than to his? If a believer's failure to conform his or her behavior to the literal meaning of a few selected verses of scripture could justify others in judging that believer and excluding him or her from the church, we LGBT Christians could make an outstanding case for your exclusion. That is not our job; and neither is it yours.

See, here's the thing—I am not terribly invested in convincing you that it is okay to be gay. I can live out my life in the joy of the Lord agreeing to disagree with you about that. If I could convince you of one thing, it would be that *the church will never be what it is meant to be, in relation to the world, until and unless we who believe in the Lord Jesus Christ get right in relation to each other*. Hateful, condemning, exclusionary theological stances, practices, and policies, aimed at unpopular sub-groups of *believers in Christ*, operate like an autoimmune disease in the Body of Christ. Parts of the Body attacking other parts of itself results in the detriment of the whole. By the miracle-working grace of God, each group makes some difference within its own sphere of influence. But the Body of Christ is meant to be more than the sum of its parts. We will not come close to the impact the church could have on the world until we all simply accept that none of us has been given the right or authority to judge another's standing before God. That right is God's alone; who, according to John 5:22-24, vested it in Jesus; who, in turn, waived it for all who believe. He *waived* the right to judge believers. He did not pass it to any of us.

You have witnessed and felt the anointing of God upon many LGBT Christians. Many pastors and priests with huge devoted followings have been used by God to minister to God's people, keeping their sexual orientation a "secret." *Much* of the music you buy and listen to at home, in your cars, and that your choirs sing in your churches, came into the world *by inspiration of the Holy Spirit* through world-renowned LGBT musicians. The Holy Spirit ministers to you through it. The Holy Spirit, *in you*, responds and witnesses to the anointing upon those who wrote it. The sermons and music of many LGBT Christians move those of you who are so inclined to clap your hands, cry, shout, and dance in the Spirit. Yet the minute those same preachers and musicians *whom God has used to minister to you* would come out and say, "I am gay," you would kick them out of your pulpits, destroy their CD's, stop singing their songs, and condemn them to Hell; unless they renounce that part of themselves.

I can neither judge nor defend their choice to minister from their closets. I do understand, though, that they did not create the system that requires them to be less than completely honest about themselves in order for the gifts of ministry that God has given them to give to world to be received by most of the Christian consumer market. You who presume to be our Accusers did that. And you perpetuate church environments that give rise to this supremely ironic phenomenon of pervasive dishonesty in the Church.

Our shared faith in Jesus Christ is our common ground. And that is the ground upon which the Lord's Table is set. We should not have to agree about everything to meet each other there. We do not have to agree about much more than Jesus is Lord. Faith in Him, love of God, and love of neighbor should provide enough common ground for us to be able to accept and embrace each other as siblings-in-Christ. It should be more than enough common ground for us to be able to worship together *openly*, in spirit and in truth, rather than in hypocritical church systems where known LGBT's are embraced as pastors, priests, preachers, musicians, and members as long as nobody asks and we do not tell.

The Church must be healed of its systemic "spiritual lupus" before we can have the full impact we are meant to have in, and upon, the world. Humility is the cure. As long as the world sees a multitude of Christians refusing to come to the Lord's table together—because one group adheres to this doctrine and another to that dogma; one group requires compliance with its code of ethics and another requires compliance with its own; and, in most churches, the consequence of non-conformity is exclusion—our impact on the world will reflect our fragmentation and be impeded by the unmitigated arrogance of some of us seeing ourselves as "holy" enough to judge others; even though Jesus, himself, declines to do that to those who hear *his* word and believe that God sent him.

I hope and I pray to be reconciled with you someday, my Accuser-siblings-in-Christ. I hope to see the day when the Apostle Paul's prayer, in Romans 15:5-7, will be our shared embodied reality:

> May the God of steadfastness and encouragement grant you to live in harmony with one another, in accordance with Christ Jesus, that together you may with one voice glorify the God and Father of our Lord Jesus Christ. Welcome one another, therefore, just as Christ has welcomed you, for the glory of God.

That is my hope and my prayer—for myself, for my LGBT siblings-in-Christ, for you, for the Church and for the world; which desperately needs us to get it right with each other, so we can be what the Church is meant to be vis-à-vis the world. But, if you cannot get there in my lifetime, if you never get there in your own lifetime, for whatever it's worth, I do not believe that God will send you to Hell for the way you have treated us, even though I am certain that the way you have treated us bears no resemblance to Jesus. You will go to Heaven for the only reason that anyone will get there—because of what Jesus did for all of us.

AN OPEN LETTER TO THE ACCUSED

We must forgive them. We need not wait for apologies from our Accusers. We should not even wait for them to stop judging and shunning us. That places the progress of our healing from the injuries they have inflicted upon us in their hands. We must lay aside the "weights" of anger, self-pity, and reliance on human beings for our validation as children of God and just forgive them; so that the spiritual channels through which God wants to speak to us, and to them through us, will be clear and open.

We must forgive ourselves, too. When we, finally, "get it" that the Accusers can hold no power over us that we do not give them, the temptation is great to blame ourselves for giving it to them in the first place. It serves no purpose to beat ourselves up about that. There are reasons why it happened, and reasons why it took so long for us to see our role in it.

We must forgive ourselves for any feelings or acts of self-hatred; and for any conscious or unconscious efforts to hurt or destroy ourselves. We must forgive ourselves for any hatred or mistreatment of others in whom we saw reflections of that which we hated in ourselves; and for sabotaging our own relationships, along with other opportunities for happiness and success. Let's make it up to ourselves by standing fast in the liberty wherewith Christ has made us free, and refusing to take on another yoke of bondage for the rest of our lives.

As LGBT Christians, we are part of a prophetic movement. We really are not in it alone, though it may seem that we are; especially to those who have been exposed only to Accuser churches. Some live immersed in, and surrounded by, the condemning theology and messages that have hurt many of us. It is an inexpressibly difficult thing to know that you are gay and that your church, your family, everyone upon whom you rely for love, a sense of belonging, and a sense of worth would more easily forgive you for killing somebody than for loving the person you love.

I was well into my thirties before I ever met anyone who acknowledged being gay. Please note—that is a very different thing from saying I had not met a gay person before then. I had. Like many of you, I went to church with several gay folks every Sunday. But none of them would ever have acknowledged it to me. So I know that feeling of "immersion" in a church culture that leaves no doubt about how you would be viewed and treated—how alone in this world you would feel—if you ever came out as gay. If this is all you have known of "church," and if "church" is all you have known, it is no wonder if you cannot imagine that there is a place for you, in Christian community, as the person you are. But there is.

Prophetic movements are never popular. By their nature, they challenge the status quo. They "call out" the majority for their establishment and perpetuation of institutions and systems that bestow unearned privilege on some, and impose undeserved stigma on others. They speak truth to power; truth that the power-holders in that system are never willing to hear.

As institutions and systems go, few are as formidable as the church in resisting prophetic movement. How ironic is that?! Most churches would rather split than change; and most *have* split before changing in response to other prophetic movements by which God corrected the church and some of its long-standing interpretations of scripture—about race and gender, for example.

Historically, prophetic movements have begun with just a few people introducing an idea into the culture that most found to be ludicrous, at best, and heretical, at worst. Typically, even the majority of the oppressed class on whose behalf God initiates the movement does not embrace it immediately. It is just too much to take in all at once; it *seems* too different from anything that has been proclaimed and heard before. But it is not really new or different, if its basis is God's radically inclusive love of all of humanity. Prophetic movements merely operate to bring the church into closer conformity with the pure, unadulterated gospel of salvation by grace through faith. That, in turn, requires re-thinking long-standing exclusionary or oppressive doctrines, dogma, and traditions; looking at them side-by-side with what Jesus said and lived, admitting the inconsistencies, and making the changes necessary for the Body of Christ to behave consistently with His Spirit. This kind of change has never happened quickly or easily, but it does happen. More and more people begin to feel the movement of the Spirit as they hear these so-called "new" ideas. As the momentum of the movement builds, those who stand to lose the most—or who live in the greatest fear of change—fight the hardest against it. But they never defeat it.

We have support, and it is gaining in momentum every day. We must believe and embrace the message that went out to LGBT teenagers following the recent multiple suicides—it does, and it will, get better. Meanwhile, we must forgive them, for our sake and for Jesus' sake. We must forgive them because we are Christians.

Now may the love of God, the peace of Christ, and the sweet communion of the Holy Spirit rest, rule, and abide with you, now and forever. Amen.

SELECTED SERMONS

THE LORD IS OUR SHEPHERD

Psalms 23 (KJV):

[1]The LORD is my shepherd; I shall not want. [2]He maketh me to lie down in green pastures: he leadeth me beside the still waters. [3]He restoreth my soul: he leadeth me in the paths of righteousness for his name's sake. [4]Yea, though I walk through the valley of the shadow of death, I will fear no evil: for thou art with me; thy rod and thy staff they comfort me. [5]Thou preparest a table before me in the presence of mine enemies: thou anointest my head with oil; my cup runneth over. [6]Surely goodness and mercy shall follow me all the days of my life: and I will dwell in the house of the LORD for ever.

John 10:22-30 (NRSV):

[22]At that time the festival of the Dedication took place in Jerusalem. It was winter, [23]and Jesus was walking in the temple, in the portico of Solomon. [24]So the Jews gathered around him and said to him, "How long will you keep us in suspense? If you are the Messiah, tell us plainly." [25]Jesus answered, "I have told you, and you do not believe. The works that I do in my Father's name testify to me; [26]but you do not believe, because you do not belong to my sheep. [27]My sheep hear my voice. I know them, and they follow me. [28]I give them eternal life, and they will never

perish. No one will snatch them out of my hand. [29]What my Father has given me is greater than all else, and no one can snatch it out of the Father's hand. [30]The Father and I are one."

The 23rd Psalm is one of the lectionary readings for today, and it jumped right out at me early last week. It is one of, if not the, most widely known and beloved passages in the Bible. Perhaps some of you, like me, were assigned to memorize it as a child, in Sunday school. I don't remember exactly when I did that, but I'm sure I could recite it, by heart, before I was 10 years old. I still recite it, by heart, every time I experience turbulence on an airplane.

Today I'm led to do a close reading of the 23rd Psalm. As familiar as some scriptures are, there's always something fresh and new to be found in them; or something of which we need to be reminded.

The Lord is my shepherd—This statement is a metaphor for a relationship. David is expressing that he is in relationship with God; which is what God wants with all of us. Then he goes on to describe that relationship.

No doubt David remembered that a good shepherd feeds and waters the sheep; guides the sheep; protects the sheep; and seeks and saves the sheep that have strayed. And, as we read this psalm today, listening for the Word in the words, we easily see the metaphor fits—because God does all of those things for us.

I shall not want—Most of us reading this statement could probably respond, "Well, I can think of a few things I want right now." David is not saying that with the Lord as our shepherd, we'll never desire or want anything. He is saying that we will never be left wanting. There's a difference.

Here, again, he is talking about his relationship with God, itself. So let's look at this from our experience in other relationships. Very few, if any of us, get everything we want in any relationship. But, that doesn't mean that the relationship, itself, leaves us wanting. To be left wanting, in a relationship, is to be unfulfilled; to feel that the relationship does not meet our needs; to feel that, whatever we may be getting out of it, it's not enough. If we are mature people and not spoiled brats, we can and do accept not getting everything we want in any relationship. But we still recognize and value those relationships where we get what we need; where we get enough not be left wanting. David is saying that, in the context of relationship with God, we will never be left wanting. We will never find that relationship unfulfilling. Because God will never fail to be, or give, enough in your relationship with God, to make it the most fulfilling relationship you'll ever have.

He maketh me to lie down in green pastures: he leadeth me beside the still waters—Phillip Keller, a pastor and author who for eight years was himself a shepherd, writes that sheep refuse to lie down if they are afraid, if there is friction with other sheep within the flock, if they are tormented by flies or parasites, and if they aren't surrounded by edible grass. There must be freedom from fear, friction, flies, and famine before sheep will lie down.

A good shepherd removes the obstacles that prevent the sheep from resting. God will progressively free us from every fear we have; and in the meantime, God will give us the courage not to be paralyzed by them.

Now, we play a part in keeping ourselves free from friction with other sheep in the flock. But God will help us with that, by giving us the will and the grace to deal peaceably with each other; to offer any apologies we owe; and the will and the grace to forgive.

The flies and parasites represent, to me, those things in our lives that trouble our spirits that we can't do anything about on our own. A sheep can't whip out a fly swatter, or a can of insect repellant to get rid of flies and parasites that drain them. And we all have situations that we just can't fix for ourselves. But the good news is that those situations give us reason to stay close to the Shepherd; and God will fix whatever needs fixing, in God's own time and way.

And the fact that God leads us to green pastures ensures that our spirits will be fed. God leads us to that which feeds us.

He restoreth my soul—This is my favorite phrase in this psalm, because it is so real and true in my life. Life can wear you out sometimes, can't it? And our souls get depleted. We accept that tests and trials will come our way. And we know that we all have to spend time in the valley; but we've never stayed down there so long before. We don't get it, because we're doing the best we can. Maybe it's a problem that drags on and on with no end in sight. Maybe it's health challenges that one doctor after another has failed to resolve.

Maybe it's a loved one for whom you've made every imaginable sacrifice who never shows a sign of gratitude. Maybe it's a goal that seems permanently beyond your reach. Whatever it is, you pray and you pray and you do the best you can until that moment when you feel your soul curl up in a ball; ready accept defeat. You can't remember the last time you felt pure joy. You can't remember the last time you felt real peace. You're sick and tired of being sick and tired, and you've done all you can, and you're too tired to think of another thing to do. You're at your lowest, and not only do you not care anymore—you don't even care that you don't care anymore.

Those are the times when we're at the end of our endurance—our lowest times; when it's not enough to know that God is there. We need God to *do* something. And those are the times when you can be certain that God will. God restores our souls; because we live in relationship with the Lord and because that the kind of Shepherd he is.

I've had times when I've gone to sleep in that condition; and I woke up with my soul restored. I'm not talking about being physically rested; that may or may not have happened. But my soul was restored; my will to live and to press on through another day was back. Sometimes God will show up to restore your soul through another person. They'll say just the exact thing that you need to hear, and it's not just something that makes you feel better; it's something that fully restores your soul. Sometimes it might be a song on the radio and its message cuts through the despair and restores your soul. God re-ignites the flame of the Holy Spirit within you. It brings your joy in the Lord back; it brings your peace back. It becomes irrelevant that your circumstances have not changed. You know, again, that one way or the other everything will be alright. You can sing, like James Cleveland, "I don't feel no-ways tired. I've come too far from where I started from. Nobody told me the road would be easy. I don't believe God brought this far to leave me." He restoreth my soul.

He leadeth me in the paths of righteousness for his name's sake—Once our souls are restored, we're ready, again, to take up our crosses and live righteous lives. Whatever our crosses may be, they don't diminish our desire to do the right thing. This is not something we can accomplish by ourselves. Like sheep, we will wander off the path, but for a loving and vigilant Shepherd to guide us back. Some of us have. Some of us here today weren't always thinking about church on Sundays. Our journeys have taken us off the highway through a few by-ways. But it's alright now because God came after us; got our attention and brought us right back to where we belong—into intimate, personal, and active relationship with God.

That's a wonderful thing. People who have never felt alienated from God may not get it. But those who have know what I'm talking about. Those who never rejected God, but were taught that God rejects you because of things you cannot change. So many are still out there; haven't set foot in a church in decades and still unwilling or afraid to come home. Those who know that experience know the value of a Shepherd that will meet you where you are—in school, at work, at home, in the nightclub—wherever you were, whatever you were doing, when you got the urge or the invitation to come home. And now look at us—back on track; back on the path of righteousness, though we had wandered away—because the Lord our Shepherd loves each of us individually; enough to do whatever it takes to bring us back.

Yea, though I walk through the valley of the shadow of death, I will fear no evil: for thou art with me; thy rod and thy staff they comfort me—That's the part that helps me on the airplanes with the turbulence. The idea of dying is a hard fact of life for some of to face. I've struggled with it, some times more than others. When the time comes, we will walk through the valley and the shadow of death. To go through anything means there's got to be something else on the other side. I read, somewhere, where somebody said that death is a spiritual event with physical implications. I believe that. It is the gateway to the next level of relationship with God—unfettered spirit to unfettered Spirit. And when we get to the valley, God will be right there waiting for us to walk through it with us; and to comfort us and calm our fears. Trust God for that; and in the meantime, live to hear the Lord say, "Well done, thy good and faithful servant."

Thou preparest a table before me in the presence of mine enemies: thou anointest my head with oil; my cup runneth over—Here is our table. I know David wasn't talking about a Communion table like this one. But looking for the Word in the words, from our vantage point as modern-day Christians, this is the table that God prepared for us. Jesus called himself our Shepherd and we who follow him his sheep. This is where we memorialize the saving work of God in the person of Jesus Christ; and accept the invitation to come home. And it occurs to me that God has prepared this table for us, as LGBT Christians, in the presence of our enemies. We share our faith in all that this table represents with all other Christians, many of whom have yet to recognize our right to be here. But apparently, that's nothing new; because God prepared a table for David in the presence of his enemies, too. It's a sad thing, but don't ever let it stand between you and this table. Listen to your Shepherd's voice. It's His table, and he invites us to it.

Surely goodness and mercy shall follow me all the days of my life: and I will dwell in the house of the LORD forever.

Thank God and Amen.

BE ROOTED IN HIM

Colossians 2:6-14 (NRSV):

[6]As you therefore have received Christ Jesus the Lord, continue to live your lives in him, [7]rooted and built up in him and established in the faith, just as you were taught, abounding in thanksgiving. [8]See to it that no one takes you captive through philosophy and empty deceit, according to human tradition, according to the elemental spirits of the universe, and not according to Christ. [9]For in him the whole fullness of deity dwells bodily, [10]and you have come to fullness in him, who is the head of every ruler and authority. [11]In him also you were circumcised with a spiritual circumcision, by putting off the body of the flesh in the circumcision of Christ; [12]when you were buried with him in baptism, you were also raised with him through faith in the power of God, who raised him from the dead. [13]And when you were dead in trespasses and the uncircumcision of your flesh, God made you alive together with him, when he forgave us all our trespasses, [14]erasing the record that stood against us with its legal demands. He set this aside, nailing it to the cross.

Today's text is a word of encouragement. The Word in the words reminds us, as Christians, to stay rooted in the pure gospel of Jesus Christ; and to live our lives in the joyful freedom of that gospel. The writer cautions us not to get caught up in human tradition, but to keep our attention focused on Christ.

Last week, we saw an illustration of how different people can see different things in the Bible. In a parable in which most of us have been taught to see a lazy, worthless servant, we saw that the poor, in some parts of the world, see that servant as a hero—a champion of justice who refused to participate in the oppression of his neighbors.

This passage from Colossians is another text that is understood, by different people, in totally different ways. So I want to remind you, as we consider this text, of the importance of context in understanding Scripture. And I want to remind you of the importance of choosing relationship over religion.

Let's look, first, at context here. The letter to the Colossians is believed to have been written between 50-55A.D. It was written to the second-generation church. The first generation of the church, particularly those under Paul's influence, had been taught to expect Jesus to return and establish the reign of God on Earth any day. When that did not happen, folks began to ask some questions; and they became vulnerable to a number of philosophies and teachings that were not things that Jesus taught. Frankly, the church was suffering a credibility crisis. Jesus hadn't returned when they were taught that he would, so some were falling away; and turning to other philosophical teachings and belief systems, and so forth. That reference, in verse 8, to "elemental spirits of the universe" is understood, by many, to be a reference to astrology, as one of the other belief systems to which some people were turning as they struggled with a crisis in their faith in the gospel of Christ. So the writer was telling the church to hold on to the pure gospel of Christ.

Now, I'll tell you how some people have misused this passage. It goes something like, "People are coming up with new ideas, like 'radical inclusiveness' and 'it's okay to be gay,' and they are pressuring the church to cave in to their agenda." But—they say—this passage in Colossians calls the church to stay rooted and grounded in Jesus, and not get caught up in human ways of thinking. In other words, they misuse this text to justify and defend their refusal to renounce their judgmental and exclusionary theologies, policies, and practices.

This passage, and the discussion surrounding it about false prophets and teachers, was never directed to any teachers of Christian faith or theology. Again, it was an effort to encourage the church, whose expectations of an imminent return by Christ were not met, not to lose faith in him and his gospel because of that and not to turn to beliefs that were deemed anti-Christian or idolatrous.

I couldn't even write for today, until I studied and prayed enough to hear the Word in the words over the noise of those old tapes in my head. But thank God for God's faithfulness to reveal the Word to those who seek him. I thought about the sermons I've heard about the church being pressured to cave in to new human ideas. And I asked myself, "Does that sound like Christ? Is that him speaking?" You will be hard-pressed to find a more radical, anti-establishment, historical figure than Jesus. All of his ideas were new! "Turn the other cheek." "The Sabbath is made for humans, not humans for the Sabbath." Paraphrasing: "Here's your new law—love God with all you've got, love you neighbor as yourself. Do this and you shall live."

The very first words of his ministry, according to Luke's gospel, are, "The Spirit of the Lord is upon me, because he hath anointed me to preach the gospel to the poor; he hath sent me to heal the brokenhearted, to preach deliverance to the captives, and recovering of sight to the blind, to set at liberty them that are bruised . . ." Jesus was all about the poor, the brokenhearted, the captives, the blind, the bruised, the marginalized, the ostracized, the last, the least, and the lost. So do we hear the Word, his Spirit, in exclusionary, oppressive interpretations of Scripture?

And this is what I mean by choosing relationship with God over religion. Religion represents mostly sincere efforts by their founders and those with power in them to tell us the meaning of whatever sacred writings they embrace. In personal relationship with God, we revere the Bible—enough to believe that God speaks through it. But in personal relationship with God, we do not allow ourselves to be spoon-fed meanings of scripture that are inconsistent with our own experience of God; and as Christians, we don't accept being spoon-fed interpretations that are inconsistent with the gospel and with the Spirit of Christ. We listen for the Word in the words of the Bible, and in the words of those who interpret, teach, and preach it. If it does not sound like Jesus, you have every right to question what they say and to reject it.

The Word that I hear in these words is "hold on to the pure gospel of Christ." Hold on to faith in *Him*. To be sure, we do need to see to it that no one takes us captive by false and deceitful teaching and human traditions. What people who abuse this biblical principle don't tell you is that most of what they believe is nothing more than their own brand of human tradition; spoon-fed to them in religious systems that don't allow for questioning and any significant degree of independent thought. That kind of church will tell us, "Know God for yourself." But what they really mean is, "Know what we tell you about God for yourself." It's not surprising that it's taking so long for *their* errors to be corrected. When we approach scripture already committed to understandings of it that have been spoon-fed to us, we aren't going to listen for the Word that speaks through the words. We won't see the resemblance between their rules and conditions for salvation and the laws that Jesus came to fulfill, so our salvation would not depend on adherence to laws and fulfillment of conditions other than faith. We aren't going to compare what we've been told a scripture means to what we understand about the radically inclusive love of Jesus Christ. We aren't even going to trust our own experience of that love, if we've allowed ourselves to be spoon-fed exclusive, oppressive theology that tells us God doesn't love us.

We must learn to distinguish between what God says and what people tell us that God said. And the way to do that, I suggest, is to do exactly what this scripture says—"As you therefore have received Christ Jesus the Lord, . . . live your lives in him, rooted and built up in him and established in the faith, just as you were taught, abounding in thanksgiving."

Now, what is "the faith, just as you were taught?" What does this mean? Some would have us to believe that this refers to the faith, just as *we* were taught, by *them*—the system of rules and codes of conduct and conditions that they have attached to being children of God in good standing with God. But that's not what this means. Here, again, interpreting scripture in context is everything.

The writer is talking about the faith that first-generation Christians were taught. He is talking about the pure gospel of Christ, which will always be consistent with the Spirit of Christ. He's talking about the faith that existed before anyone came up with the idea that you had to join a certain church, or dress a certain way, or be heterosexual, in order to have God's favor. He was reminding second-generation Christians of what first-generation Christians heard from Jesus, himself—that salvation is a gift, available to all, from the God who loves us all. It is a work of grace; for which the only requirement is faith in the power of God, who raised Jesus from the dead. He was reminding those second-generation Christians that when they were spiritually dead; destined to suffer the wages of sin, God made us alive together with Christ, when God forgave all trespasses, all sins—past, present, and future. They are, as verse 14 says, nailed to the cross of Calvary. They are all forgiven; because of the saving work of Jesus Christ. This is the faith that the early church was taught. And it is consistent with teachings and Spirit of Christ.

Anything else we've been taught—all those requirements and conditions—were added on as churches evolved and the doctrines of some grew farther and farther away from that original pure gospel-based faith. And that is why I urge you, when you hear the rhetoric, when you hear anyone preach and purport to interpret scripture for you, don't allow yourself to be spoon-fed anything by anybody—including me. If it's not consistent with the liberating, inclusive love of God, the Spirit of Christ within you will not bear witness to it.

When I read the story of Cain murdering his brother Abel, the Spirit of Christ does not bear witness to those words as truth intended to guide me in my life today. If taken literally, those words are truth, at best, in the historical sense of telling what happened back then. They are not the Christian's handy-dandy guide to swift and effective family dispute resolution.

When I read Paul's instruction to women to keep silent in the church, knowing what I know about the complete context in which those words were written, the Spirit of Christ does not bear witness to those words as truth intended to guide me in my life today. On that much, at least, even the many Accuser-female-preachers I know, and the Accuser-churches that ordain them, apparently agree with me. Those words are truth, at best, in the historical sense of being Paul's advice to that church, at that time, in their situation.

But when I read, "For I am persuaded that neither death, nor life, nor angels, nor principalities, nor powers, nor things present, nor things to come, nor height, nor depth, nor any other creature, shall be able to separate us from the love of God, which is in Christ Jesus our Lord," those words resonate within me in a way that I understand to be the Word in the words; the Spirit of Christ bearing witness to those words as truth for me, today. When we live in relationship with God, when we're listening for the Word to speak through the words, we aren't all always going to hear the exact same things. Christians have always had theological differences, beginning with the Apostles and ever since. That's why, by many estimates, there are thousands of Christian denominations in the world today. That strikes me as a sad commentary on people who are meant to be one Body. But it is what it is, for now. We've always had different, and sometimes conflicting, understandings of the Bible. I will not adhere to any that are inconsistent with the Spirit of Christ.

Therein lays the importance, for us as Christians, of getting to know Jesus. Get familiar with who He is, and what He was about while He was here bodily. The words of gospels will tell you some of it. The Word that will speak through those words will tell you more. And you'll reach the point where just like you would know if someone lied to you about someone you know intimately; just like you could say, "I know she didn't say that," or "I know he would never do that," you can do the same about Jesus. Just like you can recognize what just doesn't even sound like a person you know well, you'll get a clear sense of what Jesus was about, of His Spirit, and you'll progressively become less afraid to reject things, that you're told, that don't even sound like Him. You'll grow in courage to embrace only theology that does.

Now that you have received Christ Jesus, live like recipients of a gift. People who know they've been given a gift need not live in fear of not earning it. Live in the liberty of the original, pure gospel that Jesus preached before popes, and pastors and preachers perverted it, by attaching conditions to it. Jesus Christ is our hope. He is our salvation. Be rooted and established in him.

KNOW WHAT YOU KNOW

John 9:1-25 (NRSV):

As he walked along, he saw a man blind from birth. [2]His disciples asked him, "Rabbi, who sinned, this man or his parents, that he was born blind?" [3]Jesus answered, "Neither this man nor his parents sinned; he was born blind so that God's works might be revealed in him. [4]We must work the works of him who sent me while it is day; night is coming when no one can work. [5]As long as I am in the world, I am the light of the world." [6]When he had said this, he spat on the ground and made mud with the saliva and spread the mud on the man's eyes, [7]saying to him, "Go, wash in the pool of Siloam" (which means Sent). Then he went and washed and came back able to see.

[8]The neighbors and those who had seen him before as a beggar began to ask, "Is this not the man who used to sit and beg?" [9]Some were saying, "It is he." Others were saying, "No, but it is someone like him." He kept saying, "I am the man." [10]But they kept asking him, "Then how were your eyes opened?" [11]He answered, "The man called Jesus made mud, spread it on my eyes, and said to me, 'Go to Siloam and wash.' Then I went and washed and received my sight." [12]They said to him, "Where is he?" He said, "I do not know."

> [13]They brought to the Pharisees the man who had formerly been blind. [14]Now it was a sabbath day when Jesus made the mud and opened his eyes. [15]Then the Pharisees also began to ask him how he had received his sight. He said to them, "He put mud on my eyes. Then I washed, and now I see." [16]Some of the Pharisees said, "This man is not from God, for he does not observe the sabbath." But others said, "How can a man who is a sinner perform such signs?" And they were divided. [17]So they said again to the blind man, "What do you say about him? It was your eyes he opened." He said, "He is a prophet." [18]The Jews did not believe that he had been blind and had received his sight until they called the parents of the man who had received his sight [19]and asked them, "Is this your son, who you say was born blind? How then does he now see?" [20]His parents answered, "We know that this is our son, and that he was born blind; [21]but we do not know how it is that now he sees, nor do we know who opened his eyes. Ask him; he is of age. He will speak for himself." [22]His parents said this because they were afraid of the Jews; for the Jews had already agreed that anyone who confessed Jesus to be the Messiah would be put out of the synagogue. [23]Therefore his parents said, "He is of age; ask him." [24]So for the second time they called the man who had been blind, and they said to him, "Give glory to God! We know that this man is a sinner." [25]He answered, "I do not know whether he is a sinner. One thing I do know, that though I was blind, now I see."

As I was seeking inspiration for a Word for this morning, the ninth chapter of John got my attention. I read it, left it, and kept coming back to it until, as I read I started seeing messages imbedded in this story. I want to share what I see, for us as disciples of Christ, in this account.

A man, whose name is not given, had been blind from birth. Apparently, everyone in the area knew that. When Jesus and His disciples encountered the man, the disciples asked Jesus who had sinned—the man or his parents—to cause his blindness? Jesus responded that neither the man nor his parents had sinned. The Lord said that the man was born blind so that God's glory might be revealed in him.

> *Not everything bad that happens to us is the result of sin. Sometimes, what looks like misfortune or punishment, is simply the journey we're called to take, and the means whereby God will be glorified through us.*

No sooner had the man been healed than he was confronted by his neighbors and townspeople. Though he had lived among them all his life, some could not believe it was him. They argued, among themselves, some saying, "It's him!" and others saying, "Nah, that's somebody that looks like him."

> *When the grace of the Lord touches us, and changes us, some people won't believe it at first.*

This man spoke up and told his neighbors, "I am the man." Then the people wanted to know, "Well how were your eyes opened? How is it that you can see?"

> *Once we've had a transforming encounter with Christ, we can expect occasions to arise when we will called upon to explain what has happened to us.*

So he told them, "The man called Jesus made some mud, spread it on my eyes, and told me where to go wash it off. When I did, I received my sight."

> *Sometimes, all that stands between us and the deliverance we're seeking is an act of obedience.*

Still not convinced that what they saw before their eyes was possible, the crowd brought the healed man to the Pharisees. And the Pharisees asked him how he received his sight. The man told the story again, "Mud on my eyes, washed in Siloam, now I can see."

Again, sometimes, all that stands between us and the deliverance we're seeking is an act of obedience.

Would you believe they called his parents?! They *still* didn't believe that this was the same man who had been blind from birth. So they asked his parents, "Is this your son, who you say was born blind? How then does he now see?" And his parents said, "Let us put it to you this way—We know he's our son. And we know he was born blind. But we don't know how he can see now! He's grown, ask him yourself."

The reason God needs us to tell others about what God has done in our lives is that no one, not even the closest people to us, can tell our stories the way we can.

Well, they called the healed man before the Pharisees a second time, and this time they tried to get him to denounce Jesus. They were stuck on the fact that whatever had happened had occurred on the Sabbath. So they said, "Give glory to God! We know this Man, [meaning Jesus] is a sinner."

The Enemy of our souls will try to make us doubt our own experience with the Lord, to deny what He has done for us, and to recoil from opportunities to witness for Him. And, sometimes, this pressure will be presented in the name of God.

To appreciate the healed man's dilemma, we must recall that by the time of this incident, unfavorable attention was already being turned toward Jesus. The religious establishment of the day were building a case against Him. He had lost his temper in the Temple and poured out their money and overturned their tables. He was gaining popular attention and approval for miracles He'd performed. The Samaritan woman from the well was running all over the place shouting, "Come see a Man!" He'd healed the man at the pool of Bethzatha on another Sabbath day—by the **5th** chapter of John, we're told that the Lord's persecution was already underway. Even the healed man's parents were cautious and sent the Pharisees back to their son to let him speak for himself; because they knew that anyone who confessed Jesus to be the Messiah would be thrown out of the synagogue in disgrace.

So the healed man simply responded, "I do not know whether He is a sinner. One thing I do know, that though I was blind, now I see."

It does not matter what we don't know, as long as we remember what we do know, and stand on it.

I had that driven home to me, several years ago, in a way I'll never forget. When my sons were about 12 and 8 years old, I took them to a water park, somewhere near Greensboro I think. It has a lot of rides and activities, a lot of which involve riding or playing in water. They had this thing, like a huge pool, maybe the length of a football field. It had water in it and some sort of machine or engine that generated tall waves in the water. Each wave would start at one end of the pool and rise and fall all the way across. Then the water would recede and the wave pattern would start again at the far end of the pool.

Well, of course the boys wanted to get into this wave pool. I wasn't going to let them go in without me—don't ask me why because I can't swim—but I fancied myself to be their protector, so either we all were going in or none of us were. So I watched the thing for a while, and people were playing in it, and there were kids and adults, and it looked like a fairly simple matter to simply jump as the waves approached they'd move on down the pool.

We got in, and the very first time a wave hit me it knocked me off my feet. Keep in mind, I had no intention of getting my face wet. But there I was, on the floor of the pool, and as the rest of the wave swept over my head, I freaked out. I had all these thoughts going through my mind, the most frightening of which was, "I'm much heavier than the boys. Did the wave sweep them under, too?" I prayed for God to help me; to let somebody see that I was in trouble; to, at least, save my children, if not me. I was on the floor of the pool thrashing and praying, when, over the noise of the wave engine, the laughter of the other people in the pool, who were apparently oblivious to my impending doom, and the roar of my own blood rushing through my brain, somehow I was able to hear my sons' high-pitched, pre-adolescent voices yelling in unison, "MOMMEEEEE, STAND *UP*!!!"

One more time—sometimes, all that stands between us and the deliverance we're seeking is an act of obedience.

I opened my eyes and saw four child-sized feet planted firmly on the bottom of the pool beside me, so I followed the two sets of skinny little legs up to the surface and I stood up. You see, in my panic, I'd forgotten the one thing I knew about the pool before I got in—that the wave would recede as soon as it hit me. It had, so I'd been fighting for my life in water that came up to just about an inch below my knees. All I had to do was listen to my children—whom I was in there to protect—remember the one thing I knew, and stand up.

It wasn't easy for the healed man to stand by his experience with Christ; to stand on the one thing he knew. He had told his interrogators, several times, about the mud and washing. His parents had told them, "Yes, this is our son who was blind." At one point, the man had suggested that Jesus was a prophet. They didn't buy that. They continued to grill him and badger him about exactly what Jesus had done to him. And they had done their best to get him to denounce Jesus in order—they said—to glorify God. This man was under pressure to find some way to pacify the Pharisees, by refusing to take a stand for Christ, based on his experience of what the Lord had done for him. But when they forced him to make a choice, he said (paraphrasing): "I DON'T KNOW how He did it. I don't know WHAT He is. I don't know where He came from; I don't know where He went; and I don't know where He is at the moment. And I'll tell you something else I don't know—I don't know of any other person, since the beginning of the world, who could do what He did for me. And I don't know how He could have done it, if He was not sent from God. I only know one thing, Mr. Pharisee, as I stand here *looking* at you; but this one thing I do know—though I was blind, now I see!!!

God grant us the grace and the courage to know what we know through our own experience of Christ's touch. Sometimes that's all we're going to have. Sometimes other people just won't understand. Some of them have been taught, for too long, that what we claim in Christ Jesus is not even available to us. Some may refuse to believe us, or if they ever do, it may take time. Even among other believers, *sometimes among the closest people to us*, we won't get the affirmation of our journey that we expect all the time. And, most of the time, there will be a lot more that we don't know than there is that we know. Nevertheless, God grant us the strength of our convictions to stand on the one thing we know.

The blind man in this story was rewarded for his stand in the best possible way. As his parents had feared, his confession that Jesus was sent by God did result in his being driven out of the synagogue. But Jesus heard about that, and when He did, the scripture says Jesus found the man, and fully revealed Himself to the healed man as the Messiah.

And that's how it works. Discipleship requires us to be willing to stand for Christ, even under difficult circumstances; even in the face of skepticism. But the more faithful we are in doing it, the more fully Christ reveals Himself to us.

What's the one thing you know? We probably all have, at least, one thing—one moment; one experience; because of which we KNOW that we've been touched by Christ. For the healed man, the one thing he knew was, "though I was blind, I see." For someone else it may be, "though I was sick, I'm well." Another's testimony might be, "though I was heartbroken, I've got joy." And another might say, "though I was addicted, I'm delivered." "Though I was in despair, I have hope." "Though I was tormented, I have peace."

I'll tell you the one thing I know, and I know it, not because my parents taught it to me—though they did—and not because it's in the Bible—though it is. I know this, for myself, because the Holy Spirit has made it a personal revelation and made it real to me. The one thing I know is "For God so loved the world that God gave God's only begotten Son that **WHO-SO-EVER** believeth in Him shall not perish, but have everlasting life." I know that "whosoever" includes us.

CALLING ALL CRACKED POTS

2 Corinthians 4:5-10 (King James Version):

[5]For we preach not ourselves, but Christ Jesus the Lord; and ourselves your servants for Jesus' sake.
[6]For God, who commanded the light to shine out of darkness, hath shined in our hearts, to give the light of the knowledge of the glory of God in the face of Jesus Christ.
[7]But we have this treasure in earthen vessels, that the excellency of the power may be of God, and not of us.
[8]We are troubled on every side, yet not distressed; we are perplexed, but not in despair;
[9]Persecuted, but not forsaken; cast down, but not destroyed;
[10]Always bearing about in the body the dying of the Lord Jesus, that the life also of Jesus might be made manifest in our body.

The Apostle Paul says, " . . . we have this treasure in earthen vessels . . ." Let's start with putting this statement in a broader context than our reading to see what Paul is talking about. The 3rd chapter of 2 Corinthians ends with Paul discussing God's plan of salvation in comparison with how God related to humanity through Moses. In Moses' time, he was the only one who was allowed in the immediate presence of God. The light of God's glory shone so brightly upon Moses that, when he would come down from the mountain and from the presence of God, he would wear a veil to keep the people from seeing the bright light of God's glory upon him.

Paul says that those days are over. The life, death, and resurrection of Jesus changed everything about God's relationship with humanity. No more human mediators standing between us and God. No more veils to keep us from seeing the glory of God for ourselves. We live in personal relationship with God. Because of the gift of the Holy Spirit, God is in us. So we can get glimpses of the glory of God ourselves; in good times and bad; because wherever God is, God's glory is also.

The treasure that Paul refers to, in verse 7 of our reading, is identified in verse 6 as "the light of the knowledge of the glory of God." So the first question, for me, was "what, exactly, is meant by the glory of God here?"

The Greek word for glory; the word that Paul used in the original text, is translated literally as "opinion or reputation." So many scholars define the glory of God by reference to God's character or attributes. God is omnipotent (all powerful). God is omniscient (knows all things). God is omnipresent (everywhere). God is love. So I conclude that the knowledge of the glory of God has something to do with knowing God's character and reputation; and believing that God is, indeed, all-powerful; all-knowing; present everywhere; and loving.

But I don't think that's all of it; because I don't think Paul is talking about *intellectual* knowledge of the glory of God here. I think he's talking about knowledge in the sense of knowing what we know from experience. In other words, the treasure that we have been given is not just knowing *about* God's power, presence, knowledge, and love, in the abstract. The treasure is the *experience* of God's power, presence, knowledge, and love in the specific and personal context of our everyday lives. The treasure is the experience of the glory of God; of seeing God live up to God's reputation, as God actively works in our lives.

We experience the glory of God at those times when we know that we know that we know that something greater than ourselves is at work; and as people of faith, we know that that "something greater" could only be God. Sometimes we know it as it's happening. And sometimes we need the 20/20 vision of hindsight to see God's glory in our lives. So, sometimes, we look back at some event or situation, and we know then, without doubt, that God worked in our favor at that time. Something we didn't understand suddenly makes perfect sense. We see God's exercise of power; we see that God was present with us; we see that God knew something that we didn't know; and we see God's amazing grace and love. We see that there is, and always was, a plan; that God does, indeed, work everything together for our good—in short, we see the glory of God working in our lives.

Now this does not mean we're immune to pain and trouble in our lives. And it does not mean that we can be perfect. God placed the treasure of the knowledge of God's glory in earthen vessels. The symbolism here should not be missed. In Paul's day, they didn't have the kind of storage containers that we have today. Foodstuffs and other household supplies were stored in vessels. And it was a status symbol to have fancy and ornate vessels, of all sizes and shapes, from tea cups to huge vases to jewelry boxes to canisters for oil and grain, made of bronze, and silver, and gold and decorated with precious gemstones.

But those without money and status owned earthen vessels. Clay jars and pots made with some dirt and some water and molded by hand into vessels to hold the household supplies and whatever valuables they had. Earthen vessels were not valued as highly as those made of silver and gold. They were not symbols of status or wealth. They would crack and leak and had to be taken to the potter, who would fill in the cracks and re-fire them to keep them functional.

But here's the thing—those fancy gold and silver and bejeweled vessels in the palaces of the rich were often empty. They were just there for decoration. They had no function except to look good on the outside. The earthen vessels weren't much to look at on the outside. But you couldn't look at the outside and see the value of what was on the inside.

We are God's earthen vessels. People may look at what they see on the outside, but only God knows what's on the inside. That's why, when Satan taunted God, and said that Job would curse God if God allowed Satan to take away Job's wealth, God was able to say, with confidence, "No he won't." And when Job held on to his faith in God after losing everything he owned, Satan said, "Well, let me strike his family. He'll curse you then." And God said, "No, he won't." And Job kept holding on after his family was gone, and

Satan said, "Well, it's only because you won't let me touch his body! If you let me at his body, he will curse you and die." And God said, "No, he won't." Because God knew what Job had in him, because God put it there.

A while later, God sent Samuel to Jesse's house to anoint the next king of Israel. And Jesse lined up seven of his eight sons; all but the youngest. And Samuel looked them over one by one, convinced each time that this must be the one God had chosen. But God said, "No, no, no, no, no, no, and no." Now, Samuel knew what God had told him, so he asked Jesse, "Do you have any more sons?" And Jesse sent for David, and [paraphrasing], Samuel was like, "You say what? This scrawny, feminine-looking, little shepherd boy?" But God told Samuel to anoint David; because God knew what God had put in him. Now, David's an interesting case. Because if Samuel had had a crystal ball, and could have known some of egregious sins that David would commit, he might have thought that God had just made God's first mistake. But God knew what God put in David; and no sin, fault, or shortcoming on David's part could negate that. God knew that in the end, the treasure in that flawed, fallible, earthen vessel would yield a collection of psalms that would minister to millions of people for thousands of years.

We are earthen vessels. It doesn't matter that we may not be perfectly shaped; or that we may crack from time to time. We live in personal relationship with our Potter. God has put a treasure in us—the knowledge of the glory of God working in our lives. This is one case where knowledge is power. Paul goes on to say, "We have this treasure in earthen vessels, that the excellency of the power may be of God, and not of us." In other words, God places this treasure in flawed, fallible human beings so that when God moves and works in us, among us, and through us, we don't get confused and think we did it ourselves. God put the treasure in earthen vessels precisely so that all who see our light and our power would know that it comes from God; that it does not originate with us.

We often talk about our need to have faith in God. Today, I'm led to turn that around and tell you that God has faith in you. Sometimes all we need to believe in ourselves is to know that someone has faith in us; and God does. God's faith is never misplaced, because it is based on what God knows God put in us. Often, we don't even know all that God has put in us until we need it. We go through things and that's how we see that we have strength we didn't know we had; courage we didn't know we had; more faith than we thought we had; a greater capacity to love than we knew we had. But God knew it was in you all the time, because God put it there.

I want to leave you with two take-away thoughts this morning. The first is: "no flaw in any vessel negates the value and power of what God put in it." We all have flaws. If there's anyone who can't see one flaw in him/herself, I hate to break it you—but, oops, there it is!

Your second take-away thought for today is personal; and I can only give you the beginning of it; the Holy Spirit will finish it for you. Go to your listening place, inside, and finish this sentence: "God has faith in me to . . . ." Whatever you hear in your heart, as the end of that sentence for you, trust that the reason God has faith in you to accomplish it is that God knows what God put in you.

COME DOWN FROM YOUR SYCAMORE TREE

Luke 19:1-10 (NRSV):

He entered Jericho and was passing through it. [2]A man was there named Zacchaeus; he was a chief tax collector and was rich. [3]He was trying to see who Jesus was, but on account of the crowd he could not, because he was short in stature. [4]So he ran ahead and climbed a sycamore tree to see him, because he was going to pass that way. [5]When Jesus came to the place, he looked up and said to him, "Zacchaeus, hurry and come down; for I must stay at your house today." [6]So he hurried down and was happy to welcome him. [7]All who saw it began to grumble and said, "He has gone to be the guest of one who is a sinner." [8]Zacchaeus stood there and said to the Lord, "Look, half of my possessions, Lord, I will give to the poor; and if I have defrauded anyone of anything, I will pay back four times as much." [9]Then Jesus said to him, "Today salvation has come to this house, because he too is a son of Abraham. [10]For the Son of Man came to seek out and to save the lost."

Today, I'm led to lead us in quiet reflection on the nature of relationship with the Lord. I chose the story of Zaccheus as our starting point, because I see some important elements in this incident that give me great comfort and joy when I reflect on them.

Zaccheus was a tax collector. In our recent Bible and Homosexuality study, we talked about how important it is, for purposes of hearing the Word in the words of the Bible, to have an understanding of the social, cultural, and historical settings in which the words were written. Here, it's important to know that, back in those days, tax collectors were considered to be despicable vermin. Considering how most of us feel about the I.R.S., maybe things haven't changed much in that respect. In any case, Zaccheus was very rich, because he benefitted from an extremely corrupt system. He acquired his wealth by keeping a portion of the money that he collected from his neighbors, most of whom were poor, for the Roman government. So he was seen as a traitor to his own community; a sell-out to a system that was oppressive to those around him, because he cared only about himself and money.

As Jesus was approaching Jericho, the word got out that He was on his way; and a large crowd—probably most of the town and surrounding areas—rushed out to meet him. Zaccheus, being a bit on the short side, climbed a tree so he could see Jesus. And when Jesus saw him there, He told Zaccheus to scurry on down out of that tree, because Jesus was going to stay at his house that day.

Well, the people grumbled. Of all the people who had poured out into the streets to welcome Jesus into their town, why in the world would he choose to take up with the most despised sinner in town?

I see two possible reasons why Jesus picked Zaccheus out of that crowd. But before I get to those, I want to be sure that it registers that Jesus chose Zaccheus, not the other way around. It's not likely that Zaccheus' goal was to actually meet Jesus, or even to speak to him, because he chose to position himself *above* the crowd by climbing a tree. So it would seem that he was only trying to get a good look at Jesus; maybe just a glimpse as he walked by, surrounded by all twelve of his disciples. But, when Jesus reached the tree in which Zaccheus was perched, he looked up. I doubt that was an accident. He looked up into the branches and leaves of a sycamore tree; and he saw Zaccheus, and called him, by name—"Zacchaeus, hurry and come down; for I must stay at your house today."

That excites me! Some might say that's because I need to get a life. But this excites me, because I hear the Word in these words.

The Holy Spirit speaks to us today, through this passage, and the Word in the words is life-transforming.

Here's the first reason that I believe that Jesus chose Zaccheus: I believe that Jesus knew everything about Zaccheus. He knew he was a tax collector. He knew he was despised by those around him. But Jesus knew so much more than that. He knew what no one else in that crowd, or in the world could know—Jesus knew his heart. Jesus knew exactly how Zaccheus would respond to an encounter with him. Scripture says that Zaccheus hurried down out of that tree, happy to welcome the Lord into his house.

Here's one of the take-away thoughts for today—God does not, and has never, judged us according to the same criteria by which people judge us. We must remember that; and we must trust that God, and God alone, knows our hearts. People can see whatever they see, and can compare us to whatever standard they use to judge us. But, in the first place, no one has any business judging anyone's standing before God at all; by any standard. That's God's business, and God's alone.

And secondly, people do not have access—they cannot see or know—the most important part of us, in the eyes of God—our hearts; our spirits. Some people, for whatever reason, may appear to us to be uncaring, or angry, or difficult personalities and when you get to know them, you might discover a heart of gold; maybe a wounded heart of gold, but a heart of gold nonetheless. Others may present themselves as pious and holy and smile in your face but when that façade is cracked, it reveals a mean, ugly, and unrepentant foul spirit. People can fool us, for better or for worse. Only God has access to what is real and true, in our innermost being, and *that* is the basis upon which God calls us into relationship with Godself.

We see it all through the Bible, time and time again, Old Testament and New—God called and used Moses, a murder; Rahab, a prostitute; David, an adulterer and a murderer; Saul, later known as Paul, a vicious persecutor of Christians; Peter, an impulsive hot-head—God has always reached right on past those who believe themselves to be righteous by their own standards to seek out, choose, and call those whose hearts God knows are open to relationship with God, Godself. God knew Zaccheus' heart was open to the transformative power of an encounter with the Lord.

The second reason I believe that God chose Zaccheus was because Zaccheus was in a position, and had the resources, to bring a little more justice into his corner of the world. The thing that jumps out at me here is that Jesus never told Zaccheus he had to stop being a tax collector be saved. I hope you hear the Word in those words. Jesus never told Zaccheus he had to change a thing. It was Zaccheus who volunteered to give away half of his wealth and to repay anyone who he had defrauded four times what he cheated them out of. And, though Scripture does not tell us this, I think it's a fair assumption that, from that day on, Zaccheus became the first just and honest tax collector in Jericho. And, if that's true, Zaccheus' encounter with the Lord, his transformation resulted in the transformation of an unjust system and in blessings and benefits for his entire community.

I hope you hear the Word in the words here. God does not call us into relationship with God just so we can feel good. To be called into relationship with God is to be called to do justice; to work for justice, in our community and as far as we can reach. We are all positioned, individually and collectively, to make a difference in somebody's life. Please hear this, it's the second take-away thought for today—Just like Zaccheus, we are all positioned, individually and collectively, to make a difference in the lives of those around us. My prayer is that God will not let any of us rest until we are fully committed to discerning and doing whatever it is God's will for us to do to promote justice, healing, and reconciliation with God in our sphere of influence.

You won't find this in the Scripture, but I'm going to tell you what came to me as I meditated on this passage this week. I wondered if one reason that Zaccheus climbed that tree, instead of trying to get close to Jesus, might have been that he didn't feel worthy of anything more than glimpse of him. Sometimes as I meditate on scriptures, God leads me to put myself in the place of the characters in the story. That's one of the ways—I believe—God speaks the Word through the words. And I thought about how Zaccheus surely knew that he was a despised person in the community. And often we internalize what people tell us about ourselves. And, if we feel despised, if we've been told, for example, that we're unacceptable to God, no matter how hard we try to reject that judgment, sometimes, it creeps into our consciousness and just hangs on there.

And when that happens, sometimes that internalized judgment might lead us to be willing to settle for just a glimpse of the Lord from a distance, like high up in a sycamore tree. We might consider ourselves blessed—enough—just to have a church to come to where people aren't looking at us funny or shunning us because of those judgments with which we still wrestle inside.

I can remember, years ago, when I was in that place; happy to sit in my sycamore tree; content with being at the margin of the church I attended. I had gotten far enough along in my journey to believe that God loved me; but I hadn't healed enough from Bible abuse to feel worthy of a close and active relationship with God. When God led me to MCC, where I felt free and welcome to get involved, participate, and offer God my gifts in service to the church, at first, I hesitated to get involved. Part of it was I was just happy and relieved to find a church where I didn't have live with their version of "don't ask, don't tell." But if I'm to tell the whole truth, the other part of it was the result of internalized judgment; a feeling that I should be grateful just to be there.

I actually used to say that if I could just get to heaven, I wouldn't ask God any questions. I wouldn't be worried about how many stars would be in my crown. I didn't even have to have a crown. I'd be happy just to make it in. But over time, I realized that that feeling was a product of a deep-seated feeling of unworthiness to be called into active service of God. I was perched in my own sycamore tree; content with just knowing I would not get kicked out.

Knowing that you're judged negatively can have impacts like that, that we aren't even aware of—until we are. But I hope you hear God saying, today, that it's time to climb down out of our sycamore trees. It's time to shake off the self-imposed limitations we've placed on how God can use us, in God's service, to bear witness to the reality of our status as full-fledged, first-class children of God and members of the body of Christ. Everybody else in that crowd in Jericho may have despised Zaccheus. But Jesus, himself, called him down out that sycamore tree and invited himself into Zaccheus home and his heart. Jesus didn't give a flying fig what others *thought* of Zaccheus. Jesus *knew* him. He knew his heart.

He knows your heart, too. And He still is not influenced by what others think, because *He knows* what they can never know. He has heard every prayer you've prayed. He has seen every tear you've shed. He has felt your pain and he is not influenced by what others think or say—he says, "*Hurry* down out your sycamore tree, for I want to come stay with you today." Let's do it.

DO JUSTICE, WALK HUMBLY, BE KIND

Micah 6:1 (NRSV):

Hear what the LORD says: Rise, plead your case before the mountains, and let the hills hear your voice. [2] Hear, you mountains, the controversy of the LORD, and you enduring foundations of the earth; for the LORD has a controversy with his people, and he will contend with Israel. [3] "O my people, what have I done to you? In what have I wearied you? Answer me! [4] For I brought you up from the land of Egypt, and redeemed you from the house of slavery; and I sent before you Moses, Aaron, and Miriam. [5] O my people, remember now what King Balak of Moab devised, what Balaam son of Beor answered him, and what happened from Shittim to Gilgal, that you may know the saving acts of the LORD." [6]"With what shall I come before the LORD, and bow myself before God on high? Shall I come before him with burnt offerings, with calves a year old? [7] Will the LORD be pleased with thousands of rams, with ten thousands of rivers of oil? Shall I give my firstborn for my transgression, the fruit of my body for the sin of my soul?" [8]He has told you, O mortal, what is good; and what does the LORD require of you but to do justice, and to love kindness, and to walk humbly with your God?

Today's text is a familiar one in which we find God, through the prophet Micah, calling the people of God to answer for a controversy that God has with them. This specific passage does not tell us precisely what the people had done, or failed to do, to bring their relationship with God to this point. We find in the 2nd and 3rd chapters of Micah the evidence of their breach of fidelity to their covenant relationship with God. Briefly summarized, we find that the people lacked a sense of social justice. They were stuck in complacency that prevented them from hearing God's message. Their civic and spiritual leaders alike had abdicated their responsibility to be standard bearers who would lead God's people in righteous living.

And so it happens that God confronts the people with their failures in chapter 6; calling on the mountains, the foundations of the earth—and by implication everything located in between—to hear and bear witness to God's case against God's people and to the people's response.

Several factors have contributed to a widespread impression that Israel is now being called to task for the violation of God's laws. The fact that the biblical writer here employs a metaphorical lawsuit as the literary device for conveying this information certainly, and understandably, contributes to that interpretation. God's call for justice, widely understood in our day to be an essentially legal concept, adds to the ease with which we might see this text as being about laws and their violation.

Indeed it would seem that the respondent to God's indictment—the speaker in verses 6 and 7 of the text—assumed that God was upset about some failure to keep the letter of the law as evidenced by the question, "With what shall I come before the LORD?" after which the respondent proceeds to posit possible sacrificial offerings of increasing value with which to appease God. This prompts Micah to begin *his* response, in verse 8, with "He has told you, O mortal, what is good." Micah's response thus shifts the focus from the essence of the respondent's question—what does God what *from* us?—to the essence of the answer which, I would suggest, may accurately be understood as a statement of what God wants *for* us.

"He has told you, O mortal, what is good." Here, the good is not as much for God, as *for God's people*. The prophet says God requires God's people to do justice, love kindness (some translations say "love mercy"), and to walk humbly with our God. These are not legalistic prescriptions; they are relational parameters. They suggest that God's greatest concerns regarding God's people revolve around our relationships with God and with other people. These same core concerns—relationship with God and with other people—resonate in Jesus' statement of the greatest commandments—to love God with heart, soul, mind, and strength and to love our neighbors as ourselves.

It must remain a priority for us, as Christians, to flesh out these three requirements and allow them to guide and inform our interaction with the larger society that we are in, but not of. But I believe we can't hope to get it right vis a vis the world until we get it right in relation to each other. So I'm led to invite us to consider what doing justice, loving kindness and mercy, and walking humbly with our God might look like in the specific context(s) of our own communities of faith. And in that regard, I offer that:

1. We're called to practice responsive living; that is, living in response to an unbroken memory of ourselves as recipients of the unmerited grace of God. The purpose of vv. 4-5 of the text is to remind God's people of God's grace and goodness toward them. The clear implication is that remembering should inspire responsive living; not mere observance of legalistic rules or ritualistic worship. Remembering should inspire a responsive way of being, particularly in relation to one another.
2. We must renounce those prejudices, fears, and animosities that have resulted in the proliferation of intentionally homogenous communities of faith, rather than congregations that accurately reflect the demography of the communities in which they are situated and of the Body of Christ. In other words, beloved siblings-in-Christ, I'm suggesting that we must stop coddling ourselves and telling ourselves that it's okay that we prefer to worship with "our own kind," in our own preferred styles and traditions to the exclusion of fellowship with different others. Those isms and phobias that lead us to marginalize and reject different others who believe the gospel and embrace Jesus as Lord are not of God.
3. Finally, I invite us to be intentional about, and committed to, desegregating and diversifying our congregations and embracing all who name Jesus as Lord as the siblings in Christ that they are. I'm

not looking to any other governmental leaders for whatever justice I hope to see in my lifetime. Talk of a kinder and gentler America notwithstanding, I'm not holding my breath waiting for love of kindness and mercy to materialize, manifest, and flow to me from Washington, DC. But it breaks my heart when I can't find those things in a church. It's distressing and sad to know that there are churches all around this Bible belt where I would not be welcomed to join, much less allowed to fulfill the ministry to which I am called.

And, in this regard, as I address this audience most largely comprised of pastors-, ministers-, and Christian educators-in-training, I feel compelled to tell you that we are the leaders whose call and task it is to promote social justice, kindness, mercy, and humble walking with God in the Body of Christ. I don't imagine, for one minute, that being a prophet is easy. Nonetheless, we are the ones who must be the Micah's of our day and refuse to allow tradition, habit, prior socialization, salary or job security concerns, our mamas, our grandmamas or any other distractions to deter us from preaching this truth—what God desired in Micah's day, and reiterated in the person of Jesus Christ, remains what God requires of God's people today. We are the prophetic witness to the world and that obliges us to show the world what it means to "do justice, and to love kindness, and to walk *humbly* with [our] God." May it be so, in Jesus' name. God bless you.

THE TOP 10 WAYS TO RECOGNIZE FREE PEOPLE

Romans 8:1-4

There is therefore now no condemnation for those who are in Christ Jesus. [2]For the law of the Spirit of life in Christ Jesus has set you free from the law of sin and of death. [3]For God has done what the law, weakened by the flesh, could not do: by sending his own Son in the likeness of sinful flesh, and to deal with sin, he condemned sin in the flesh, [4]so that the just requirement of the law might be fulfilled in us, who walk not according to the flesh but according to the Spirit.

I'm going to share a few thoughts with you, today; inspired by Holy Spirit, the scripture I just read, today's theme, "I am Free," and by—David Letterman.

My thoughts are about, "The Top 10 Ways to Recognize Free People." Now to narrow that down a little, I'm talking about people who understand what Paul is saying in our reading; and have stopped living as if the law of sin and death still governs us. I'm talking about people whom the Son has set free. So let's call ourselves free-indeed people.

The top ten ways to recognize free-indeed people:

#10. Free-indeed people are honest people. Jesus said, "You shall know the truth; and the truth shall make you free." Well, the flip side of that coin is, "You shall tell the truth, and that will keep you free." Lies and secrets bind the spirit. They put us in prison, to the extent that they prevent us from being our whole, real self around those people to whom we lie, and from whom we keep secrets. Which brings me to a closely related point —

#9. Free-indeed people are free everywhere, all the time. We don't turn our freedom on in the club, and off at work. We don't turn it on at one church, and turn it off at another church. We don't turn it on when we're with our friends and turn it off when we're around our families. Free-indeed people are free all the time, wherever we go.

#8. There's nothing in free-indeed peoples' closets but their clothes, their shoes, and a few other miscellaneous items. I think that one is self-explanatory.

#7. Free-indeed people forgive everybody for everything. Just like lies and secrets, grudges bind the spirit. I know some injuries are harder to forgive than others. Even in those cases, free-indeed people know, from the moment we are insulted or injured, that we won't be completely free again until we forgive. If it's any comfort to you, keep yourself reminded that you're not doing it for them. You're doing it to keep yourself free. Forgive everybody; for everything.

#6. Free-indeed people are neither legalistic nor licentious. There are those who tell us that if we're not one we're the other. That is not true. You hear that from the same folks who say, "Know God for yourself," but really mean, "Know what we tell you about God for yourself." Free-indeed people are not afraid to think for ourselves; to seek truly personal relationship with God; and to trust our own experience of God. We have been delivered from the bondage of theological legalism. But that does not mean we are licentious. Licentiousness is the knowing and intentional abuse of God's grace. It is a conscious choice to live in disregard of our understanding of God's will for us; an attitude like,

"Grace covers all my sins, so I'll sin all I want to." Our freedom is not about disregard of God's will for us. Our freedom is God's will for us. Free-indeed people don't abuse God's grace. We understand it. And from that understanding springs forth gratitude that ignites a burning desire to discern and do the will of God, for the glory of God.

#5. Free-indeed people have been healed of our religion-based neuroses about sex. We are delivered from the extremes of compulsive promiscuity and involuntary abstinence required by mandates to be "non-practicing." We have discovered that, sometimes, practice does indeed make perfect. More importantly, free-indeed people have experienced that sex between people whom God has joined together is, in fact, a spiritual experience with physical manifestations. It is good; and that's okay. We seek God's guidance in discerning sound ethical parameters, and within those parameters, we enjoy the gift of our sexuality.

#4. Free-indeed people are not afraid to let go of the guilt and shame that have bound them. I remember a time when I was afraid to be free. I was scared to have peace. I was scared to not feel guilt. Because I was afraid that the moment I didn't feel any more guilt about being a same-gender-loving woman, that would mean I'd been given over to a reprobate mind.

And I remember, clearly, the night that the Spirit laid that lie to rest for me. The Spirit said, "You're terrified of being free of guilt and shame because you think that when you no longer have those feelings, it will mean you are a reprobate. But reprobates don't pray like you do. They don't love me like you do. Reprobates don't have the anointing on them that I have placed on you. They have no concern about serving or pleasing me. In short, reprobates do not care whether they are reprobates." Free-indeed people have learned that we do not have to hold on to shame and guilt, to keep us on the right side of the line between redeemable and reprobate. We are redeemed already and forever by the saving work of God in Christ Jesus.

#3. Free-indeed people love to praise God. We may not all do it the same way; and that's fine. How ever our praise is manifested, we refuse to quench the Spirit. Some may cry, some may laugh, some may shout and dance, some may clap their hands, and some may turn inward and praise God in ways that the rest of us can't see. It's all good; because when God graces us with an outpouring of the Holy Spirit in our midst, free-indeed people have more important things to do than look around to see what others are doing. We're busy receiving our blessing. So when you find yourself in a situation where the Holy Spirit is pouring out blessings and calling for praise from God's people, I'm not going to tell you what you should do. All I'll suggest is if you're happy and you know it—do something. Free-indeed people praise God for setting us free.

#2. Free-indeed people want everyone else to be free, and are willing to be used by God toward that end. That's one reason we have to leave our closets at home; and come out as both as Christians and as LGBTQI's or as allies. I've heard Bishop Flunder say, "Free people, free people." And that's what I'm saying here. It's important for that to be part of our ethic because bound people are still busy binding people. Oppressors are busy oppressing. A lot of good people are still doing nothing to alleviate suffering and promote social justice. I really believe that it is inherent in the state of being free-indeed to want to see everyone set free.

And the #1 way to recognize free-indeed people is — Free-indeed people understand the meanings of the words "grace" and "gift." This understanding is crucial to loving ourselves into liberation; because feelings of unworthiness are the root cause of difficulty in loving oneself. Whether it's because of things we've done, things we've failed to do, critical caretakers, oppressive theology, or anything else—identify the true source of your feelings of unworthiness and you will have identified the mountain standing between yourself and liberating self-love. But when we truly understand the meanings of the words "grace" and "gift" that mountain has no choice but to move out of our way. Grace is, by definition, "unmerited favor" and a gift, by definition, does not have to be earned. When I was in grade school, my teachers would ask me to use my vocabulary words in a sentence, to demonstrate that I understood what they meant. I got your sentence: "For by grace you have been saved through faith, and that not of yourselves; it is the gift of God . . ." The words "grace" and "gift," in that sentence render worthiness a non-issue. Free-indeed people understand that our freedom did come at a price. But Jesus paid it all.

So, my siblings-in-Christ, "Stand fast, therefore, in the liberty wherewith Christ has made us free, and be not entangled again with anyone's yoke of bondage."

God bless you.

THE YOU THAT GOD KNEW

Jeremiah 1:4-10 (NRSV):

> [4]Now the word of the LORD came to me saying, [5]"Before I formed you in the womb I knew you, and before you were born I consecrated you; I appointed you a prophet to the nations." [6]Then I said, "Ah, Lord GOD! Truly I do not know how to speak, for I am only a boy." [7]But the LORD said to me, "Do not say, 'I am only a boy'; for you shall go to all to whom I send you, and you shall speak whatever I command you, [8]Do not be afraid of them, for I am with you to deliver you, says the LORD." [9]Then the LORD put out his hand and touched my mouth; and the LORD said to me, "Now I have put my words in your mouth. [10]See, today I appoint you over nations and over kingdoms, to pluck up and to pull down, to destroy and to overthrow, to build and to plant."

I'm going to offer a few thoughts, for your consideration, around the topic, The You That God Knew. As background, I'll share that this thought was given to me as I read the passage from the first chapter of Jeremiah in which God tells the prophet, "Before I formed you in the womb I knew you, and before you were born I consecrated you; I appointed you a prophet to the nations." I'd read and heard the passage many times. But on this particular reading, the phrase, "I knew you" just, sort of, jumped out at me in that way that the Holy Spirit works with me to plant the seed that will eventually yield a word for me to preach. I became enthralled with that phrase, "Before I formed you, I knew you." I *knew* you. I knew *you.*

I have long believed that we are embodied spirits; that there is more to us than flesh and blood. My understanding of Jeremiah 1:5 and of the 139th Psalm, among other scriptures, makes it easy for me to believe that God knew me, too, in spirit, before I was born and will continue to know me, in spirit, after I die. So I read those words, "Before I formed you, I knew you." And I found myself wondering, "Who was I then?" And I wondered, "To what extent have those people and things that have been influential in my life since I was formed in my mother's womb brought about change in that spirit-being that was the me that God knew?

I want to make explicit a belief and premise, that is my starting point. I believe that God created the me that God knew exactly as God intended. And I believe that God created the you that God knew exactly as God intended. Drawing on the reading from Jeremiah, I suggest that God loved us as God knew us, and that God had plans for us, as God knew us, and placed calls on our lives before we had life, as we know it now. So I'm starting with the proposition that it is a good and desirable thing to find your way back, or to step fully into being, the you that God knew before.

Well, that naturally led me to the question, "Before what?" I can only speak from my own experience, but my prayer is that as I share my exploration of this thought, God will trigger your own applications of the idea that will resonate and speak to you.

The first thing that necessarily came up, for me, was the impact of my upbringing as a Pentecostal fundamentalist. The Pentecostal part wasn't the problem. The Holy Spirit is our friend. It's the fundamentalist part that can mess you up. Anytime you accept and internalize a detailed and rigid formula, of human origin, designed to set parameters to which you must conform, to be in relationship with God, you are at high risk of becoming someone other than the you that God knew, before.

I've come to believe that the driving force behind fundamentalism is fear. So I've gone from resenting fundamentalists to genuinely feeling sorry for them because I think that they have completely forgotten the "them" that they were before. They have forgotten that there was a time when they didn't need anyone to tell them who

God is and what God is to them. They have forgotten that there was a time when they didn't need to conform to a long list of specific do's, don't's, what's, how's, when's, where's, with whom's, and under what circumstances, to live in peaceful relationship with God. Fundamentalists have forgotten that there was once a time when it never would have occurred to them that God could do anything but love them.

Fundamentalists have forgotten all of that; so they live in fear of God, and of not getting it right, not *being* right, not being sure of everything, and of making mistakes that will cost them their souls. But I offer to you, tonight, the word that was given to me—the you that God knew was not afraid of God. The you that God knew was not afraid of yourself either; of being yourself as God created you. The you that God knew was secure in God's love for you. *Be the you that God knew*.

So I continued to meditate on this idea of the me that God knew, before. And I went on with my life; with a heightened attentiveness to anything that could shed some light on all of this for me.

And I had the opportunity, a few weeks ago, to meet and spend some time with Bishop Yvette Flunder and her life-partner Mother Shirley Miller. I was seated beside Mother Miller at a reception, in Bridgeport, CT, following a service where Bishop Flunder had preached. And Mother Miller and I talked for over an hour and, as God would have it, our conversation triggered me to share with her this idea that had been marinating in my spirit about the "you that God knew." Mother Miller immediately lit up and ran with it. What I got from what she said is that most of think of life as a journey forward, with the end-point or destination being some place or state that we've never experienced before. But on a deeper, spiritual level, she suggested that maybe life, as we know it, is a journey *back* to where we started in relation to God; maybe our goal should be to *remember* what we've already known and experienced of God at some point; maybe we would be well-served to try to remember and re-claim, as *spirit*-beings who live as embodied human beings only for an appointed time, who we were created and born to be in this world.

Now, they did teach me something like that in seminary. This idea is reminiscent of a portion of Origen's cosmology and anthropology.

But I probably missed most of it while I was taking notes and trying to figure out how to spell "A-Pok-a-tas-Tay-sis." Even now, I've spelled it phonetically, just to be able to say it without stumbling. So Mother Miller made a lot more sense to me. And I left her that day thinking that, "Maybe the task of *discerning* God's will for us is, in some way, the task of *remembering* God's will for us; or at least, remembering and staying mindful of who we are as God knew us from the beginning."

Life presents all of us—individually and collectively—with situations and challenges that can operate to steer us off our intended course, and inhibit us from being who God created and knew before we were exposed, or subjected, to those things. But I encourage you, today, to be the you that God knew.

To my Accuser siblings-in-Christ, be the you that God knew before you learned fear and before some of you discovered that judging others makes you feel better about yourself.

To anyone who has been wounded by fundamentalist influences—be the you that God knew in *relationship*; before you knew there was any such thing as religion.

To my transgendered siblings-in-Christ—be the you that God knew before you had a body of any kind; before incongruous chromosomes and misguided socialization pressed you to be other than who you are in spirit.

To my LGBT siblings-in-Christ who are sitting on your gifts and letting God's call on your life go to voice-mail, because you're still not convinced that you're worthy of God's anointing—be the you that God knew when you sang, "Yes, Jesus loves me" without a shadow of a doubt that it's true. If God consecrated the you that God knew as a singer, sing to glory of God. If God consecrated the you that God knew as a prayer warrior, pray without ceasing as the Spirit leads. If God consecrated the you that God knew as a healer, lay your hands on those to whom God leads you that they may be healed for the glory of God. If God consecrated the you that God knew as a prophet, prophesy; speak truth to power and deliver your soul. If God consecrated the you that God knew as a preacher, preach the Word and don't let anyone tell you you're not worthy of your calling, when God found you worthy enough to anoint you to do it.

To any and all whose challenges and struggles I haven't called out, but who know that something in your life has led to an inauthentic adaptation of some kind—be the you that God knew before whatever that was.

And last, but not least, to all of God's beloved, *love the you that God knew*. That's the you that God created. That's the you that God loves. That is the you who God knew every, single thing about; when God chose to send *that* you into the world for God's own purposes; determined before you born. Be the you that God knew—before.